Real-Time Applications with Node.js: Build Scalable Real-Time Systems

A Step-by-Step Guide to Building Real-Time Apps with Node.js

MIGUEL FARMER

RAFAEL SANDERS

Table of Content

TABLE OF CONTENTS

INTRODUCTION

Real-Time Applications with Node.js

The landscape of application development is evolving rapidly. Users expect more interactive, engaging, and dynamic experiences. Gone are the days when applications were static or based on slow, request-response interactions. Today, real-time applications are driving the modern web, from live chats and social media feeds to real-time gaming and Internet of Things (IoT) systems.

At the heart of many of these applications lies **Node.js**, a powerful, event-driven runtime that excels at handling high concurrency and real-time communication. **Node.js** provides an ideal environment for building real-time applications due to its non-blocking I/O and asynchronous programming model. However, developing real-time systems introduces unique challenges—handling constant data flow, ensuring low latency, and dealing with scalability issues across distributed systems.

This book is designed to guide you through the process of building scalable and efficient real-time applications using **Node.js**. It provides you with the knowledge, tools, and strategies to develop everything from basic real-time features like WebSockets to more advanced architectures that include microservices, IoT integrations, serverless platforms, and edge computing. Whether you're building a real-time chat app, a multiplayer game, or an IoT-powered system, this book will provide you with the foundational knowledge and practical skills necessary to bring your ideas to life.

Why Real-Time Applications Matter

The demand for real-time applications has never been higher. With the advent of modern web technologies, real-time communication has become a cornerstone of user experience. Users expect to interact with applications that are instantaneous, updating information live without the need for page refreshes or manual inputs.

Examples of real-time applications are everywhere:

- **Social Media**: Live updates to your feed, comments, likes, and notifications are all real-time experiences.
- **Messaging Platforms**: Applications like WhatsApp, Facebook Messenger, and Slack rely on real-time messaging to keep users connected instantly.
- **Gaming**: Multiplayer games like Fortnite, Apex Legends, and Rocket League depend on low-latency, high-performance communication to ensure a seamless experience for players worldwide.

- **IoT Systems**: From smart homes to industrial automation, IoT systems collect and process real-time data, allowing immediate responses based on the data received.

For all these systems to function smoothly, real-time data transmission must be handled efficiently. In real-time applications, a delay of even a few milliseconds can disrupt the user experience. This book focuses on building applications that process, transmit, and respond to data instantly, creating an uninterrupted and engaging user experience.

Why Node.js for Real-Time Applications?

Node.js has become a popular choice for building real-time applications due to its asynchronous, non-blocking nature. This means that Node.js can handle many connections simultaneously without waiting for one process to complete before starting the next, making it highly efficient for handling real-time data.

Here's why Node.js is particularly suited for real-time applications:

- **Event-Driven Architecture**: Node.js is inherently designed to be event-driven, allowing it to handle real-time events like user interactions, device updates, or network messages efficiently.
- **Scalability**: Node.js's non-blocking I/O model makes it ideal for handling a large number of simultaneous

connections, which is essential for real-time applications that require constant communication (e.g., a multiplayer game with hundreds of players).

- **Large Ecosystem**: With an extensive library of modules available through **npm (Node Package Manager)**, developers can quickly integrate WebSockets, messaging protocols, authentication systems, and databases to build complex real-time applications.

From handling user input in real time to providing notifications, **Node.js** excels in providing both the performance and flexibility needed to deliver real-time functionality with minimal delay.

What You'll Learn

This book covers a broad range of topics that will equip you with the skills to develop robust real-time applications using Node.js. Here's a look at the key areas we'll dive into:

1. **Core Real-Time Concepts**: We begin by exploring the key concepts behind real-time applications— understanding what real-time communication is, how it works, and why it's so crucial for modern applications. This foundational knowledge will set the stage for more advanced topics later in the book.

2. **Setting Up Real-Time Communication**: Learn how to use technologies like **WebSockets** and **Socket.IO** to

establish real-time communication between the client and server. These tools are foundational for building live-updating features in your application.

3. **Building Real-Time Features**: Through practical examples, you'll learn to implement real-time features such as messaging systems, live notifications, and interactive multiplayer games.

4. **Scalability and Performance**: As your real-time application grows, you'll need to scale efficiently. This book will teach you how to build scalable systems using **Docker**, **Kubernetes**, and microservices architectures, ensuring your app can handle high traffic and user interactions seamlessly.

5. **Integration with IoT**: One of the most exciting areas for real-time applications is **Internet of Things (IoT)**. You'll learn how to collect and process real-time data from IoT devices using Node.js, enabling you to build systems that interact with the physical world in real-time.

6. **Advanced Topics**: As we move deeper, we will explore **serverless computing**, **edge computing**, and the future of real-time protocols, offering insight into how these technologies will shape the next generation of real-time applications.

7. **Real-World Examples**: Throughout the book, you will work on real-world projects, from building a **chat application** and **real-time multiplayer game** to setting

up an **IoT-powered system** for monitoring and controlling devices.

Who This Book Is For

This book is aimed at developers who are interested in building real-time applications using **Node.js**. Whether you're a beginner to Node.js or an experienced developer looking to expand your knowledge of real-time systems, this book provides clear, practical examples and step-by-step instructions to help you succeed.

Specifically, this book is ideal for:

- **Web developers** who want to integrate real-time communication features (such as messaging, notifications, or live updates) into their applications.
- **IoT enthusiasts** interested in working with real-time data from IoT devices, and who want to learn how to process and respond to that data using Node.js.
- **Game developers** who wish to create multiplayer games with real-time features like player interactions and game state synchronization.
- **Backend developers** who want to learn how to handle real-time communication, scaling, and deployment for high-traffic applications.

How to Use This Book

This book is designed to be hands-on, with practical examples and detailed explanations. Each chapter builds on the previous one, guiding you through the process of designing and deploying real-time applications. Here's how you can use this book effectively:

- **Start from the beginning** if you're new to real-time applications, or **jump to specific chapters** that focus on the areas you want to learn more about.
- **Follow along with the examples** and try to implement the features on your own. Coding along with the examples will reinforce your understanding and improve your skills.
- **Experiment with the projects**. Once you're comfortable with the basics, try extending the projects to include new features, test them with real-world traffic, or deploy them to a cloud environment.

Next Steps

After completing this book, you'll have a deep understanding of how to build real-time applications using **Node.js** and how to integrate advanced features like **IoT**, **scalability**, and **microservices**. But the journey doesn't end here. The world of real-time applications is constantly evolving, with new technologies and methodologies emerging. Staying current is key to being successful in this field.

You should continue to:

- **Explore new tools and frameworks** in the real-time ecosystem, such as **WebTransport**, **GraphQL Subscriptions**, and emerging protocols.
- **Contribute to open-source real-time projects** and collaborate with other developers to keep learning and improving.
- **Stay updated** with the latest advancements in **cloud technologies**, **edge computing**, and **serverless architectures**, all of which are shaping the future of real-time systems.

The future of real-time applications is vast and full of opportunities. With the knowledge you gain from this book, you'll be well-prepared to create the next generation of real-time, scalable, and interactive applications.

Welcome to the world of real-time development with Node.js. Let's get started!

CHAPTER 1

INTRODUCTION TO REAL-TIME APPLICATIONS

What Makes an Application "Real-Time"?

In the simplest terms, a real-time application is one that reacts to events or changes as they occur, providing users with an immediate response. This immediate feedback loop is what differentiates real-time applications from traditional ones. Real-time apps are designed to handle interactions and data updates without significant delays, which is crucial in scenarios where timing is essential.

There are different types of real-time applications based on the timing constraints:

- **Hard real-time systems**: These applications must guarantee that they complete a task within a strict deadline. Missing this deadline could lead to critical failure (e.g., air traffic control systems, embedded systems in medical devices).
- **Soft real-time systems**: While these systems strive for quick responses, missing a deadline doesn't cause a catastrophic failure. It may just lead to a slight

degradation in performance (e.g., video streaming, online gaming).

In everyday terms, real-time means that the system is constantly monitoring data and ready to process it as soon as it changes or an action is taken.

Real-World Examples of Real-Time Applications

Real-time applications are found in nearly every industry, as they are crucial for handling live data and providing instant feedback. Here are a few examples:

1. **Messaging and Chat Applications**
   o Apps like WhatsApp, Slack, and Facebook Messenger allow users to send messages that appear instantly on the recipient's screen without delays.
   o These apps maintain an open connection between the client and server, using protocols like WebSockets to transmit messages as soon as they are sent.

2. **Online Gaming**
   o Multiplayer games like Fortnite, PUBG, and Minecraft require real-time interaction between players. The game state must constantly update to reflect the actions of multiple players in real time.

3. **Collaborative Tools**
   o Tools like Google Docs and Microsoft Office 365 enable multiple users to edit the same document simultaneously, with changes appearing instantly for everyone.

4. **Financial Applications**
   o Stock market apps or trading platforms such as Robinhood or E*TRADE provide real-time price updates and allow users to make trades based on live market data.

5. **Video Streaming**
   o Services like YouTube Live or Twitch deliver real-time video content, enabling viewers to watch events as they happen and interact with streamers through live chat.

6. **Social Media Feeds**
   o Facebook, Twitter, and Instagram show real-time updates to the news feed, showing posts, likes, and comments as they happen.

These applications rely on constant data flow and immediate updates to provide the user with a seamless, real-time experience. Without this functionality, the user experience would be much less interactive, and users may feel disconnected.

Why Choose Node.js for Real-Time Apps?

Node.js is an ideal choice for building real-time applications due to several key factors:

1. **Non-Blocking, Asynchronous I/O**
   Node.js is built on a non-blocking, event-driven architecture. This means that it can handle multiple I/O operations (such as reading files, making network requests, or interacting with databases) concurrently without waiting for one to complete before starting the next. This behavior is crucial for real-time apps, which require immediate responses and can't afford to be delayed by slow operations.

2. **Single-Threaded Model**
   Node.js operates on a single-threaded event loop, which allows it to handle many concurrent connections efficiently. Since most real-time applications involve numerous users simultaneously interacting with the system, this model helps avoid the complexity of multi-threading and ensures low latency communication.

3. **Real-Time Communication with WebSockets**
   Node.js excels at managing WebSocket connections, which are ideal for real-time communication. WebSockets enable bi-directional communication between the client and server over a single, persistent connection. This is much more efficient than traditional

17

HTTP request/response models for real-time interactions. Node.js has libraries like Socket.IO that make it simple to implement WebSockets in your applications.

4. **Scalability**

Node.js is highly scalable and can handle many connections at once. This is essential when dealing with applications that require real-time interaction from thousands or even millions of users, such as in gaming or social media. With Node.js, you can scale vertically (adding more powerful hardware) or horizontally (adding more servers) without much hassle.

5. **Large   Ecosystem   and   Libraries**

Node.js has a vast ecosystem of libraries and modules, many of which are specifically designed for building real-time applications. Whether you're handling database queries, implementing WebSockets, or managing authentication, there's likely a well-documented package available that simplifies your development process.

6. **JSON   as   Data   Format**

Since Node.js uses JavaScript, working with JSON (a lightweight data-interchange format) is seamless. JSON is commonly used in real-time applications to transfer data between the client and server, and the integration with JavaScript makes this process extremely efficient.

7. **Active   Community   and   Resources**

The Node.js community is large, active, and constantly

evolving. This ensures that you have access to a wealth of resources, tutorials, and examples for building real-time applications. Moreover, the community frequently updates existing libraries and tools, ensuring compatibility with the latest technologies.

In conclusion, Node.js provides all the key features necessary to build fast, scalable, and efficient real-time applications. Its event-driven architecture, WebSocket support, scalability, and strong ecosystem make it one of the most popular choices for real-time app development today.

CHAPTER 2

SETTING UP YOUR DEVELOPMENT ENVIRONMENT

Installing Node.js and npm

Before you can start developing real-time applications with Node.js, the first step is to install Node.js and npm (Node Package Manager) on your local machine. Both are essential for developing, running, and managing Node.js applications.

Step-by-Step Guide to Installing Node.js and npm:

1. **Download Node.js:**
   - Visit the official Node.js website: https://nodejs.org.
   - On the homepage, you'll see two download options:
     - **LTS (Long Term Support):** Recommended for most users as it's the stable version.
     - **Current**: Contains the latest features but may have some instability.

- o Choose the LTS version for a more reliable experience, especially when working on production-level projects.
- o Download the installer for your operating system (Windows, macOS, or Linux).

2. **Install Node.js:**

- o Run the installer you downloaded. The process will vary depending on your operating system:
  - On **Windows** and **macOS**, simply follow the prompts in the installation wizard.
  - On **Linux**, you can install Node.js using a package manager like `apt` (for Ubuntu) or `yum` (for Fedora).
- o After installation, Node.js and npm will be installed together as npm is bundled with Node.js.

3. **Verify the Installation:**

- o After installation is complete, open your terminal or command prompt and run the following commands to verify the installation:
  - To check Node.js version:

```bash

node -v
```

  - To check npm version:

```bash
```

21

```
npm -v
```

    o   If the installation was successful, you should see version numbers for both Node.js and npm.

Setting Up a Project Structure

Once you have Node.js and npm installed, it's time to set up your project. A well-organized project structure is essential for maintaining and scaling your application as it grows.

Basic Project Structure for Real-Time Apps:

bash

```
my-real-time-app/
├── node_modules/        # Automatically created
by npm to store dependencies
├── public/              # Static files (HTML,
CSS, images)
│     └── index.html
├── src/                 # Application source
code
│     ├── controllers/   # Business logic for
your app
│     ├── models/        # Database models
│     ├── routes/        # Routes to handle HTTP
requests
```

```
|     └── services/         # WebSocket logic and
other services
├── .gitignore              # Git ignore file to
exclude unnecessary files
├── package.json            # Project metadata and
npm dependencies
└── server.js               # Main server file (entry
point)
```

Step-by-Step Guide to Set Up the Project Structure:

1. **Create a Project Directory:**
   - First, create a new directory for your project and navigate into it:

   ```bash
   bash
   ```

   ```
   mkdir my-real-time-app
   cd my-real-time-app
   ```

2. **Initialize npm:**
   - Run the following command to initialize a new Node.js project:

   ```bash
   bash
   ```

   ```
   npm init -y
   ```

o   This command creates a `package.json` file in your project folder, which will store metadata about your project and its dependencies.

3. **Create Folders and Files:**

o   Manually create the necessary directories and files as shown in the project structure. You can create these using the terminal or your code editor.

o   Example:

```bash
```

```
mkdir  src  public  src/controllers
src/models src/routes src/services
touch server.js
```

4. **Install Dependencies:**

o   Install any necessary packages or libraries that you'll need for your real-time app, such as Express and Socket.IO:

```bash
```

```
npm install express socket.io
```

o   This will create a `node_modules` folder to store the packages.

5. **Update `package.json`:**

- o The `package.json` file will automatically update with the details of the packages you installed.
- o You can add a `start` script to run your server, making it easier to start your app with a simple command:

```json
json

"scripts": {
  "start": "node server.js"
}
```

Basic Debugging Tools for Node.js

Debugging is an essential part of the development process, especially for real-time applications where errors can disrupt user interactions. Here are a few debugging tools and techniques that will help you identify and fix issues in your Node.js application.

1. Console Logging (Basic Debugging):

- The simplest and most common debugging method in Node.js is using `console.log()` to output data to the terminal.
- For example:

```javascript
javascript
```

25

```
console.log('Hello, Node.js!');
```

- This is useful for checking variable values, confirming execution flow, and understanding the app's behavior at specific points.

2. Node.js Built-in Debugger:

- Node.js comes with a built-in debugger that can be used for step-by-step debugging.
- To start the debugger, run your app with the `inspect` flag:

```bash

node inspect server.js
```

- This will start your application in debugging mode and allow you to set breakpoints, inspect variables, and step through your code.

3. Debugging with Chrome DevTools:

- You can also debug your Node.js application using Chrome's DevTools, which provide an interactive interface for debugging JavaScript.
- To start debugging with Chrome DevTools, run your application with the `--inspect` flag:

```
bash

node --inspect server.js
```

- Then, open `chrome://inspect` in your Chrome browser and click on "Open dedicated DevTools for Node." You'll be able to set breakpoints and step through your code directly in the Chrome DevTools interface.

4. Debugging with Visual Studio Code:

- Visual Studio Code (VS Code) is one of the most popular code editors for Node.js development and offers an excellent debugging experience.
- To set up debugging in VS Code:
    - Open your project in VS Code.
    - Go to the "Run" tab on the left sidebar and click "Add Configuration."
    - Choose "Node.js" from the list of available configurations and select the file you want to debug (usually `server.js`).
    - Set breakpoints by clicking in the gutter next to the line numbers.
    - Press `F5` or click the green play button to start debugging.

5. Third-Party Debugging Libraries:

- There are several third-party libraries available for more advanced debugging in Node.js. Some of the most popular ones include:
  - **debug**: A small library that allows you to output debug information based on namespaces.
  - **winston**: A logging library that can handle various log levels, such as info, warn, error, etc.

To install debug, for example:

```bash
bash
```

```bash
npm install debug
```

Then, use it in your application like so:

```javascript
javascript
```

```javascript
const debug = require('debug')('app');
debug('This is a debug message!');
```

By setting up the correct development environment and debugging tools from the start, you'll be able to create, test, and troubleshoot your real-time Node.js applications with ease.

CHAPTER 3

UNDERSTANDING NODE.JS
FUNDAMENTALS

Node.js Event-Driven Architecture

Node.js is built around an **event-driven architecture**, which is key to its ability to handle many concurrent connections with high performance. At the heart of this design is the **Event Loop** (discussed later), but understanding how events and callbacks work is fundamental to building efficient applications with Node.js.

In an event-driven architecture, there is an **event emitter** that triggers actions based on certain events. When a specific event occurs, an associated callback function is executed. The core idea is to allow the application to perform non-blocking I/O operations and handle multiple tasks simultaneously.

Here's an overview of how it works:

1. **Event Emitters**: Node.js uses the `EventEmitter` class (available in the `events` module) to handle events. When an event occurs, the system emits the event, and a registered listener (callback function) responds to that event.

29

Example:

```javascript

const EventEmitter = require('events');
const myEmitter = new EventEmitter();

myEmitter.on('event', () => {
  console.log('An event occurred!');
});

myEmitter.emit('event');  // Output: An event occurred!
```

2. **Asynchronous Execution**: In a Node.js application, events are often triggered by I/O operations (such as reading a file, making a network request, or querying a database). Instead of waiting for one task to finish before starting the next, Node.js can trigger multiple operations in parallel. Once an operation completes, the event is emitted, and the corresponding callback is executed.

3. **Real-World Use Case**: For instance, if your app is handling HTTP requests, each incoming request can be considered an event. Node.js listens for these events and processes each request asynchronously, without blocking the server from handling other requests in parallel.

Single-Threaded Model and Non-Blocking I/O

One of the most unique features of Node.js is its **single-threaded** architecture, which allows it to handle many connections efficiently. Let's break down what this means:

1. **Single-Threaded Event Loop**:
   o Traditional web servers use a **multi-threaded** model, where each request is handled by a separate thread. This can lead to performance issues as threads are resource-intensive.
   o Node.js, however, operates on a **single thread** with an **event loop**. The event loop processes one operation at a time but can handle thousands of requests concurrently. This is possible because Node.js delegates time-consuming tasks (such as file I/O) to the system's background threads, allowing the event loop to remain free to handle new events.

2. **Non-Blocking I/O**:
   o In a traditional system, I/O operations (e.g., reading a file or querying a database) can block the execution of other code until the operation completes. This can cause delays if there are multiple I/O operations.
   o Node.js, on the other hand, uses **non-blocking I/O** to avoid this issue. When a Node.js

31

application initiates an I/O operation, it doesn't wait for the operation to complete. Instead, it continues to execute other code and only calls back the function once the I/O operation has finished.

o This allows Node.js to be highly efficient and able to handle many operations concurrently, without being bogged down by I/O delays.

Here's a simple example of how Node.js handles non-blocking I/O:

javascript

```
const fs = require('fs');

// Non-blocking file reading
fs.readFile('file.txt', 'utf8', (err, data) => {
  if (err) throw err;
  console.log(data);  // Output: File contents
});

// This line runs immediately after initiating
the read operation, without waiting for it to
finish
console.log('File read initiated!');
```

In this example:

- The file reading operation is initiated with `fs.readFile()`, but Node.js doesn't wait for it to complete before continuing. The `console.log('File read initiated!')` is printed immediately.
- Once the file reading is done, the callback is invoked, and the file content is logged.

Introduction to Callbacks and Event Loops

At the core of Node.js's asynchronous behavior are **callbacks** and the **event loop**.

1. **Callbacks**:
   - A **callback** is a function that is passed as an argument to another function and is executed once that function has completed its task.
   - In Node.js, callbacks are widely used to handle asynchronous operations. For example, when reading a file, instead of waiting for the operation to finish, you pass a callback that will be executed once the file has been read.

Example of a callback:

```javascript

const doSomethingAsync = (callback) => {
  setTimeout(() => {
```

```
    console.log('Async          operation
complete');
    callback();      // The callback is
executed once the operation is finished
  }, 1000);
};


doSomethingAsync(() => {
  console.log('Callback executed');
});
```

2. **Event Loop**:

- o The **event loop** is the mechanism that allows Node.js to handle asynchronous tasks. It constantly checks if there are any tasks in the queue and processes them one by one.
- o The event loop runs in a single thread but can process multiple operations simultaneously by delegating tasks to other parts of the system when necessary (e.g., for I/O operations).

The event loop follows a set of phases:

- o **Timers**: Executes callbacks for timers (e.g., `setTimeout` or `setInterval`).
- o **I/O Callbacks**: Executes most callbacks, including those for I/O operations.

- o **Idle, Prepare**: Internal phase used for housekeeping tasks.
- o **Poll**: Retrieves new I/O events and executes callbacks.
- o **Check**: Executes callbacks for `setImmediate()`.
- o **Close Callbacks**: Executes close event callbacks (e.g., `socket.on('close', ...)`).

This loop continues to run as long as there are tasks to handle. If there are no tasks left, the event loop exits.

Here's an example that demonstrates the event loop in action:

```javascript
console.log('Start');

setTimeout(() => {
  console.log('Timeout callback executed');
}, 0);

console.log('End');
```

Expected Output:

```sql
Start
```

```
End
Timeout callback executed
```

- Even though `setTimeout()` was called with a 0-millisecond delay, its callback isn't executed immediately. It is placed in the event queue and will only run after the main execution stack is clear, which is why `End` is printed before the `Timeout callback executed`.

How the Event Loop Works:

- The synchronous code (`console.log('Start')` and `console.log('End')`) is executed first, blocking nothing.
- The `setTimeout()` function places the callback in the event queue.
- Once the synchronous code has finished executing, the event loop picks up the callback from the queue and executes it.

Key Takeaways:

- **Event-driven architecture** means that the application reacts to events as they occur and uses callbacks to respond to these events.

- Node.js's **single-threaded model** means that the application can handle multiple connections efficiently without requiring multiple threads.

- The **event loop** handles asynchronous tasks and ensures non-blocking behavior by executing tasks only when they're ready, making Node.js suitable for high-concurrency applications.

- **Callbacks** are used to handle asynchronous operations, allowing you to perform tasks concurrently without blocking the program's flow.

Understanding these fundamentals is essential for building efficient, scalable real-time applications with Node.js.

CHAPTER 4

WORKING WITH WEB SERVERS IN NODE.JS

In this chapter, we'll cover the basics of setting up a web server in Node.js, as well as how to handle requests and responses. We'll also introduce **Express.js**, a popular Node.js framework that simplifies routing and provides powerful tools for building web servers.

Creating a Basic HTTP Server

In Node.js, you can create a basic HTTP server using the built-in `http` module. This module allows you to create a server that listens for incoming HTTP requests and sends responses back to the client.

Here's an example of creating a simple HTTP server:

```javascript
const http = require('http');

// Create a server
const server = http.createServer((req, res) => {
  // Set the response HTTP header
```

```
res.writeHead(200,          {          'Content-Type':
'text/plain' });

  // Write the response body
  res.end('Hello, world!\n');
});

// Make the server listen on port 3000
server.listen(3000, () => {
  console.log('Server          running          at
http://localhost:3000/');
});
```

Explanation:

- **http.createServer()**: This method creates an HTTP server. It takes a callback function that is executed every time the server receives a request. The callback has two parameters: req (the request object) and res (the response object).

- **res.writeHead(200)**: This sets the HTTP status code for the response. 200 means "OK."

- **res.end()**: This sends the response to the client and ends the request-response cycle.

- **server.listen(3000)**: This instructs the server to listen for incoming connections on port 3000.

When you run this script and navigate to `http://localhost:3000` in your browser, you should see "Hello, world!" displayed on the page.

Introduction to Express.js for Routing

While Node.js's `http` module can be used to build servers, it's relatively low-level and requires you to handle many things manually (like routing and middleware). This is where **Express.js** comes in. Express is a minimal web framework for Node.js that simplifies server creation, routing, and handling HTTP requests.

Installing Express: To get started with Express, you first need to install it using npm:

```bash
```

```bash
npm install express
```

Once installed, you can use it to set up a more powerful and feature-rich web server.

Creating a Simple Server with Express:

```javascript
```

```javascript
const express = require('express');
const app = express();
```

```
// Define a route for GET requests
app.get('/', (req, res) => {
  res.send('Hello, world with Express!');
});

// Start the server on port 3000
app.listen(3000, () => {
  console.log('Server          running          at
http://localhost:3000/');
});
```

Explanation:

- **express()**: This function creates an Express application (a web server).
- **app.get()**: This method defines a route for handling GET requests to the specified URL (' / ' in this case). The callback function is executed whenever a GET request is made to that URL.
- **res.send()**: This sends a response to the client. In this case, it's sending a simple text message.
- **app.listen()**: This starts the Express server on port 3000.

The code above is more concise and easier to manage than using the basic http module. Express provides many built-in features like routing, middleware support, and more.

Handling Requests and Responses

In both the basic HTTP server and Express, handling requests and responses is a fundamental part of building web applications. Let's break this down into key areas:

1. Handling Different HTTP Methods

Express allows you to handle different HTTP methods (like GET, POST, PUT, DELETE, etc.) in a more structured and readable way. Here's an example:

javascript

```javascript
const express = require('express');
const app = express();

// Handling GET request
app.get('/', (req, res) => {
  res.send('This is a GET request!');
});

// Handling POST request
app.post('/', (req, res) => {
  res.send('This is a POST request!');
});

// Handling PUT request
app.put('/', (req, res) => {
```

```
  res.send('This is a PUT request!');
});


// Handling DELETE request
app.delete('/', (req, res) => {
  res.send('This is a DELETE request!');
});


app.listen(3000, () => {
  console.log('Server          running          at
http://localhost:3000/');
});
```

- **app.get()**: Handles HTTP GET requests.
- **app.post()**: Handles HTTP POST requests.
- **app.put()**: Handles HTTP PUT requests.
- **app.delete()**: Handles HTTP DELETE requests.

Each route corresponds to a specific HTTP method, and the callback will be executed based on the type of request received.

2. Using Route Parameters

Express allows you to define dynamic routes using route parameters. These parameters are extracted from the URL and can be used in the request handling logic.

Example:

43

javascript

```
app.get('/user/:id', (req, res) => {
  const userId = req.params.id;
  res.send(`User ID is: ${userId}`);
});
```

- **:id**: This is a route parameter. When a request is made to /user/123, the value of id will be 123.
- **req.params.id**: This accesses the value of the id parameter from the URL.

3. Using Query Parameters

Query parameters are part of the URL and are typically used to send small amounts of data. Express makes it easy to work with query parameters.

Example:

javascript

```
app.get('/search', (req, res) => {
  const query = req.query.q;   // Accessing the
query parameter "q"
  res.send(`Search term: ${query}`);
});
```

- If the request is GET /search?q=Node.js, req.query.q will be equal to 'Node.js'.

4. Sending JSON Responses

One of the most common tasks in web servers is sending JSON data. Express makes it very easy to send JSON responses.

Example:

javascript

```
app.get('/data', (req, res) => {
  const data = { message: 'Hello, world!' };
  res.json(data);   // Sends a JSON response
});
```

- **res.json()**: This method sends a JSON response, which is typically used for APIs that need to send structured data.

5. Handling Errors

In real-world applications, errors are inevitable. Express provides a simple way to handle errors in your routes.

Example:

javascript

```
app.get('/error', (req, res) => {
  throw new Error('Something went wrong!');
});

// Express error-handling middleware
app.use((err, req, res, next) => {
  console.error(err.stack);
  res.status(500).send('Something broke!');
});
```

- **app.use()**: This is middleware that catches errors in your application. The error-handling middleware needs to take four arguments (err, req, res, next).
- When an error is thrown, it is passed to the error-handling middleware, where you can log it and send an appropriate response.

Summary

- **Basic HTTP Server**: You can create a simple web server in Node.js using the http module. This gives you fine-grained control over request handling but requires more manual setup.
- **Express.js**: A web framework that simplifies routing, request handling, and many common server tasks. It provides an easier way to create scalable applications.

- **Request Methods**: Express makes it easy to handle different HTTP methods such as `GET`, `POST`, `PUT`, and `DELETE`.

- **Route Parameters and Query Strings**: Express allows dynamic routes and easily accessible query parameters, making it easier to handle dynamic URLs and form data.

- **Sending JSON**: Use `res.json()` to send JSON responses, which is commonly used in APIs.

- **Error Handling**: Use middleware to handle errors gracefully, ensuring your server doesn't crash unexpectedly.

With these fundamentals in place, you can now start building more sophisticated web servers with Node.js and Express!

CHAPTER 5

WEBSOCKETS AND REAL-TIME COMMUNICATION

In this chapter, we'll explore **WebSockets**, a protocol that is critical for enabling real-time communication between clients and servers. We'll cover what WebSockets are, how to set up WebSocket servers with Node.js, and how to use them for real-time messaging applications.

What are WebSockets?

WebSockets are a communication protocol that allows for **full-duplex** (two-way) communication over a single, long-lived connection. Unlike traditional HTTP, where the client must initiate a request and the server responds, WebSockets enable real-time, bidirectional communication, allowing data to be sent and received instantly by both the client and the server.

Key Features of WebSockets:

- **Persistent Connection**: After the initial handshake, the connection remains open, allowing continuous communication between the client and the server.

- **Low Latency**: Since the connection is persistent, there's no need for constant reconnection or HTTP request-response cycles. This allows for faster data transmission.

- **Full-Duplex Communication**: Both the client and the server can send and receive messages simultaneously without having to wait for the other party to finish.

- **Efficient Data Transfer**: WebSockets use a lightweight frame format for communication, which reduces overhead and improves performance compared to HTTP-based protocols.

In WebSockets, the client first sends an HTTP request to upgrade the connection to a WebSocket connection. Once the upgrade is successful, the connection switches from HTTP to WebSocket and remains open for ongoing communication.

Setting Up WebSocket Servers with Node.js

To set up a WebSocket server with Node.js, we can use the `ws` library, which is one of the most popular WebSocket libraries for Node.js. It provides simple and efficient WebSocket support.

Step-by-Step Guide:

1. **Install the `ws` Library**:
   - First, you need to install the `ws` library via npm:

   ```bash
   bash
   ```

49

```
npm install ws
```

2. **Create a WebSocket Server**:
   o Once the library is installed, you can create a basic WebSocket server in Node.js.

Here's an example of setting up a simple WebSocket server:

```javascript

const WebSocket = require('ws');
const http = require('http');

// Create an HTTP server
const server = http.createServer((req,
res) => {
  res.writeHead(200,  {  'Content-Type':
'text/plain' });
  res.end('WebSocket server is running');
});

// Create a WebSocket server attached to
the HTTP server
const wss = new WebSocket.Server({ server
});
```

```
// Set up event listener for incoming
WebSocket connections
wss.on('connection', (ws) => {
  console.log('A new client connected');

  // Send a welcome message to the client
  ws.send('Welcome to the WebSocket
server!');

  // Set up event listener for messages
from the client
  ws.on('message', (message) => {
    console.log('Received: %s', message);
  });

  // Handle client disconnection
  ws.on('close', () => {
    console.log('Client disconnected');
  });
});

// Start the server on port 8080
server.listen(8080, () => {
  console.log('Server is running at
http://localhost:8080');
});
```

Explanation:

- `http.createServer()`: We first create an HTTP server that listens for incoming HTTP requests. Although the HTTP server itself doesn't directly handle WebSocket connections, it provides the foundational server on which the WebSocket server will run.

- `new WebSocket.Server()`: The WebSocket server is created by passing the HTTP server as an argument. This binds the WebSocket server to the same port.

- `wss.on('connection', callback)`: This event listener is triggered when a new client connects to the WebSocket server. The callback receives the `ws` object (WebSocket instance) that represents the connection.

- `ws.send()`: This sends a message to the connected client.

- `ws.on('message', callback)`: This listens for messages sent by the client.

- `ws.on('close', callback)`: This handles the event when a client disconnects.

Once the server is running, you can test it using a WebSocket client or a browser's developer tools (e.g., using the JavaScript `WebSocket` API).

Real-Time Messaging with WebSockets

WebSockets are often used for real-time messaging applications, where messages need to be sent immediately to users without the delays associated with traditional HTTP requests. Here's how to implement a basic real-time chat application using WebSockets in Node.js.

1. **Setting Up the WebSocket Server (Server-Side)**: Let's extend the previous example to build a simple real-time chat server that allows multiple clients to send messages to each other.

   ```javascript
   const WebSocket = require('ws');
   const http = require('http');

   const server = http.createServer((req, res) => {
     res.writeHead(200, { 'Content-Type': 'text/plain' });
     res.end('Real-time chat server');
   });

   const wss = new WebSocket.Server({ server });

   // Store all connected clients in an array
   const clients = [];

   wss.on('connection', (ws) => {
     console.log('A new client connected');
   ```

```
clients.push(ws); // Add new client to
the clients array

  ws.on('message', (message) => {
    console.log('Received message: %s',
message);

    // Broadcast the message to all
connected clients
    clients.forEach(client => {
      if (client !== ws &&
client.readyState === WebSocket.OPEN) {
        client.send(message); // Send the
message to other clients
      }
    });
  });

  ws.on('close', () => {
    // Remove the client from the list when
disconnected
    const index = clients.indexOf(ws);
    if (index !== -1) {
      clients.splice(index, 1);
    }
    console.log('Client disconnected');
  });
});
```

```
server.listen(8080, () => {
  console.log('Chat server is running at
http://localhost:8080');
});
```

Explanation:

- **Clients Array**: We keep track of all connected WebSocket clients in an array (`clients`). Each time a new client connects, they are added to this array.

- **Broadcasting Messages**: When a client sends a message, it is broadcast to all other connected clients. This is achieved by iterating over the `clients` array and sending the message to every other WebSocket client.

- **Client Disconnection**: When a client disconnects, we remove their WebSocket instance from the `clients` array.

2. **Setting Up the WebSocket Client (Client-Side)**: To interact with the server, we need to create a WebSocket client. Here's how to create a simple HTML and JavaScript-based client for the chat application.

```html
html
```

```html
<!DOCTYPE html>
<html lang="en">
<head>
```

55

```
<meta charset="UTF-8">
<title>WebSocket Chat</title>
</head>
<body>
<h1>Real-Time Chat</h1>
<input      type="text"      id="message"
placeholder="Type a message..." />
<button
onclick="sendMessage()">Send</button>
<div id="chat"></div>

<script>
const         ws         =         new
WebSocket('ws://localhost:8080');

// Listen for messages from the server
ws.onmessage = (event) => {
const         messageDiv         =
document.createElement('div');
messageDiv.textContent = event.data;

document.getElementById('chat').appendChi
ld(messageDiv);
};

// Send message to the server
function sendMessage() {
const         message         =
document.getElementById('message').value;
```

```
      ws.send(message);    //    Send    the
message to the WebSocket server

document.getElementById('message').value =
''; // Clear input field
    }
  </script>
</body>
</html>
```

Explanation:

- **WebSocket('ws://localhost:8080')**: Creates a WebSocket connection to the server.
- **ws.onmessage**: Event listener for incoming messages. When a message is received, it is displayed in the chat window.
- **ws.send()**: Sends the typed message to the WebSocket server when the "Send" button is clicked.

Now, when you open this HTML page in a browser and run the WebSocket server from the previous step, you should be able to send messages between multiple clients connected to the server in real time.

Summary

- **WebSockets** provide real-time, bidirectional communication between the client and server, making them ideal for real-time applications like chat apps, notifications, and live data feeds.
- In **Node.js**, you can set up a WebSocket server using the ws library to handle connections and send/receive messages.
- Real-time messaging applications can be easily built by setting up a WebSocket server and using the ws.send() method to broadcast messages between multiple clients.

CHAPTER 6

BUILDING A CHAT APPLICATION: A REAL-WORLD EXAMPLE

In this chapter, we'll create a **real-time chat application** from scratch using Node.js and WebSockets. The chat application will allow multiple users to connect to the server and send messages to each other in real-time. We will go through the entire process, from conceptualizing the app to setting up the server and implementing message broadcasting.

Conceptualizing a Simple Chat App

Before diving into the code, it's essential to conceptualize what our chat application will do:

1. **User Connections**: Users will connect to the chat server via a WebSocket connection.
2. **Real-Time Messaging**: When a user sends a message, the server will broadcast it to all other connected users instantly.
3. **User Interface**: The front end of the application will display incoming messages in real-time.

4. **Disconnections**: The app should handle user disconnections gracefully and notify others when a user has left.

The architecture of the application will be as follows:

- A **WebSocket server** will be set up on the backend using Node.js.
- The **frontend** will use a simple HTML and JavaScript interface to interact with the WebSocket server.
- The **message broadcasting** will be implemented to allow all connected users to receive each other's messages instantly.

Setting Up WebSocket for Real-Time Chat

We'll start by creating the WebSocket server with **Node.js** and **ws library**, which allows us to handle WebSocket connections. The basic structure of the server will involve creating an HTTP server and upgrading the connection to a WebSocket server, just like we did in previous chapters.

Step 1: Install Dependencies

You'll need Node.js installed on your machine. Then, install the ws library using npm:

bash

```
npm install ws
```

Step 2: Create the WebSocket Server

Now, let's create the WebSocket server.

```javascript
const WebSocket = require('ws');
const http = require('http');

// Create the HTTP server
const server = http.createServer((req, res) => {
  res.writeHead(200,        {        'Content-Type':
'text/plain' });
  res.end('Real-time chat server is running');
});

// Create the WebSocket server
const wss = new WebSocket.Server({ server });

// Array to store connected clients
const clients = [];

// Handle new client connections
wss.on('connection', (ws) => {
  console.log('A new client connected');
  clients.push(ws);  // Add the new client to the
clients array
```

```
// Send a welcome message to the new client
ws.send('Welcome to the chat!');

// Handle incoming messages from clients
ws.on('message', (message) => {
    console.log('Received     message:     %s',
message);

    // Broadcast the message to all other clients
    clients.forEach(client => {
      if (client !== ws && client.readyState ===
WebSocket.OPEN) {
        client.send(message);  // Send message to
other clients
      }
    });
  });

  // Handle client disconnection
  ws.on('close', () => {
    const index = clients.indexOf(ws);
    if (index !== -1) {
      clients.splice(index, 1);   // Remove the
client from the array
    }
    console.log('A client disconnected');
  });
});
```

```
// Start the server on port 8080
server.listen(8080, () => {
  console.log('Chat       server       running       at
http://localhost:8080');
});
```

Explanation:

- We create an HTTP server (`http.createServer`) that serves a simple message when a user visits the server.
- We use **WebSocket.Server** to create a WebSocket server, which will handle incoming WebSocket connections.
- The **clients** array stores all connected clients. Each time a new client connects, their WebSocket object is added to the array.
- When a message is received from a client, it's broadcasted to all other connected clients using `client.send()`. The message is only sent to clients that are still connected (i.e., their `readyState` is `OPEN`).
- When a client disconnects, we remove them from the `clients` array to clean up.

Step 3: Test the WebSocket Server

To test the WebSocket server, run the Node.js server:

```bash
bash
```

```bash
node server.js
```

The server should now be running on http://localhost:8080.

Implementing Message Broadcasting

Now that we have the WebSocket server set up, let's implement the **message broadcasting** feature.

1. When a client sends a message, the server will send it to all other connected clients.
2. This ensures that all users in the chat receive the same message in real-time.

The code above already includes broadcasting functionality inside the message event listener:

```javascript
javascript
```

```javascript
clients.forEach(client => {
  if (client !== ws && client.readyState ===
WebSocket.OPEN) {
    client.send(message);  // Send the message to
other clients
  }
});
```

The `forEach` loop iterates over all the connected clients and sends the message to every client except the one that sent the message (`client !== ws`). We check if the connection is open by verifying `client.readyState === WebSocket.OPEN` to ensure that we only send the message to clients that are still connected.

Setting Up the Client-Side Interface

Now that we have the WebSocket server and message broadcasting set up, let's create a simple client interface. The client will connect to the WebSocket server and display incoming messages in real time.

Step 1: Create the HTML Interface

Here's the HTML structure for the chat application:

html

```
<!DOCTYPE html>
<html lang="en">
<head>
  <meta charset="UTF-8">
  <meta name="viewport" content="width=device-width, initial-scale=1.0">
  <title>WebSocket Chat App</title>
</head>
<body>
```

65

```
<h1>Real-Time Chat</h1>
<div id="chat"></div>
<input          type="text"          id="message"
placeholder="Type a message..." />
<button onclick="sendMessage()">Send</button>

<script>
    // Establish a WebSocket connection to the
server
    const          ws          =          new
WebSocket('ws://localhost:8080');

    // Display a message when the WebSocket
connection is established
    ws.onopen = () => {
        console.log('Connected to the WebSocket
server');
    };

    // Display incoming messages in the chat
    ws.onmessage = (event) => {
        const          messageDiv          =
document.createElement('div');
        messageDiv.textContent = event.data;

document.getElementById('chat').appendChild(mes
sageDiv);
    };
```

```
// Send the message to the WebSocket server
function sendMessage() {
  const          message          =
document.getElementById('message').value;
  if (message) {
    ws.send(message);

document.getElementById('message').value = '';
// Clear input field
  }
}
</script>
</body>
</html>
```

Explanation:

- **new WebSocket('ws://localhost:8080')**: This line establishes a WebSocket connection to the server running on localhost on port 8080.

- **ws.onmessage**: Every time a message is received from the WebSocket server, this event listener adds the message to the #chat div on the page.

- **sendMessage()**: This function sends a message to the server when the user types a message and clicks the "Send" button.

Step 2: Test the Chat App

- Open the `index.html` file in multiple browser tabs or different browsers.
- As users type and send messages, they will be broadcast to all other connected users in real time.

Summary

In this chapter, we've:

- **Conceptualized** a simple real-time chat app.
- **Set up the WebSocket server** using Node.js and the `ws` library.
- **Implemented message broadcasting**, ensuring that all connected clients receive each message sent by any user.
- Created a **simple frontend** that allows users to send and receive messages in real time.

This basic chat app serves as the foundation for more complex real-time applications, such as group chats, private messaging, and interactive collaboration tools.

CHAPTER 7

UNDERSTANDING EVENT EMITTERS IN NODE.JS

In this chapter, we'll dive into **EventEmitters**, one of the core components of Node.js that allows you to build event-driven applications. Event-driven programming is a major paradigm in Node.js, and understanding how it works will help you develop more scalable, efficient, and responsive applications.

Working with Node.js EventEmitter

In Node.js, the **EventEmitter** class is part of the **events** module, and it's the cornerstone of asynchronous programming in Node.js. The EventEmitter allows you to handle and manage events, making it possible for your application to respond to specific actions or occurrences as they happen.

1. **Importing the EventEmitter Module:** To use EventEmitter, we first need to import the events module:

javascript

```
const EventEmitter = require('events');
```

2. **Creating an Instance of EventEmitter:** You can create an instance of the EventEmitter class, which will allow you to register event listeners and emit events.

javascript

```
const myEmitter = new EventEmitter();
```

3. **Listening for Events:** To react to specific events, you use the **on()** method to attach event listeners. These listeners will be executed when the corresponding event is emitted.

javascript

```
myEmitter.on('event', () => {
  console.log('An event occurred!');
});
```

In this example, we are listening for the 'event' event. When the event is emitted, the callback function will run and log the message 'An event occurred!'.

4. **Emitting Events:** To trigger an event, you use the **emit()** method. This method fires the event and triggers all listeners attached to that event.

javascript

```
myEmitter.emit('event');
```

This will trigger the `'event'` event and execute any attached listeners. In this case, the output will be:

```
csharp
```

```
An event occurred!
```

How Event-Driven Programming Works in Node.js

Event-driven programming is based on the concept of events and event handlers. The event loop in Node.js listens for events and runs code in response to these events. Let's break this down:

1. **Event Loop**: The event loop is a fundamental part of Node.js. It runs continuously and checks for any events that have been emitted. Once an event is emitted, the event loop triggers the associated listeners, executing the code provided in those listeners.

2. **Non-Blocking Operations**: Node.js is non-blocking, meaning it doesn't wait for a task (such as reading a file or querying a database) to complete before moving on to the next task. Instead, Node.js emits an event once an operation completes and triggers the corresponding listener to handle the result. This allows Node.js to handle many tasks concurrently without blocking the execution of the application.

3. **Callbacks and Events**: In Node.js, much of the application flow is determined by events and callbacks.

When an event is triggered, the callback function attached to that event is executed. This is the basis for asynchronous programming in Node.js.

4. **Examples of Node.js Events**:

   o **HTTP Events**: When handling HTTP requests, Node.js emits events like `request`, `response`, etc.

   o **File System Events**: When working with files, Node.js emits events like `open`, `close`, `data`, and `end`.

   o **Custom Events**: You can define your own events based on the needs of your application.

Using Event Emitters in Real-Time Applications

Event-driven programming is especially useful in **real-time applications** because it allows your application to respond to user interactions or system events as soon as they occur. Below are some examples of how you might use EventEmitters in a real-time Node.js application:

1. **Real-Time Chat Application**: Imagine a chat application where each time a user sends a message, the server emits a `message` event, and all connected clients listen for that event to receive and display the message in real time.

Here's a basic example of how EventEmitters could be used in a real-time chat server:

```javascript
const EventEmitter = require('events');

// Create a new EventEmitter instance
const chatEmitter = new EventEmitter();

// Array to store connected clients (for
simplicity)
const clients = [];

// When a new client connects, add them to
the clients array
function onClientConnect(client) {
  clients.push(client);
  console.log('A    new    client    has
connected!');
}

// When a message is received, emit a
'message' event
function onMessageReceived(message) {
  console.log('Message         received:',
message);
```

```
  // Broadcast the message to all connected
clients
  chatEmitter.emit('message', message);
}


// When a 'message' event is emitted, send
the message to all clients
chatEmitter.on('message', (message) => {
  clients.forEach(client => {
    client.send(message);
  });
});


// Example usage
const client1 = { send: (message) =>
console.log('Client 1 received:', message)
};
const client2 = { send: (message) =>
console.log('Client 2 received:', message)
};


// Simulate client connections
onClientConnect(client1);
onClientConnect(client2);


// Simulate a message being sent
onMessageReceived('Hello, everyone!');
```

Explanation:

- o We create a custom `EventEmitter` instance (`chatEmitter`).
- o We emit a `message` event whenever a message is received, which triggers all connected clients to receive and display the message.
- o This is a simple example, but it demonstrates how you can use `EventEmitter` in a real-time scenario, such as broadcasting messages to all connected clients in a chat app.

2. **Real-Time Notifications**: In a real-time notification system, each time a user triggers an event (such as receiving a new message, a like, or an update), an event can be emitted to notify the user. For example:

javascript

```
const EventEmitter = require('events');
const notificationEmitter = new
EventEmitter();


// Function to simulate sending a
notification
function            sendNotification(user,
notification) {


notificationEmitter.emit('newNotification
', user, notification);
}
```

```
// Listener to handle new notifications
notificationEmitter.on('newNotification',
(user, notification) => {
  console.log(`Sending    notification    to
${user}: ${notification}`);
});
```

```
// Simulate sending notifications
sendNotification('John Doe', 'You have a
new message!');
```

Explanation:

- A newNotification event is emitted each time a new notification is triggered.
- All listeners to this event will act on the event, allowing the application to respond immediately to the incoming notification.

3. **Real-Time Data Updates (e.g., Stock Ticker)**: In a stock trading application, real-time stock prices can be updated and broadcasted using EventEmitters. For example, when a stock price changes, an event can be emitted to notify all clients of the new price.

```javascript
const EventEmitter = require('events');
const stockEmitter = new EventEmitter();
```

```
// Function to simulate stock price update
function updateStockPrice(stock, price) {
  stockEmitter.emit('stockPriceUpdate',
stock, price);
}

// Listener to handle stock price updates
stockEmitter.on('stockPriceUpdate',
(stock, price) => {
  console.log(`Stock:   ${stock}   |   New
Price: $${price}`);
});

// Simulate stock price updates
updateStockPrice('AAPL', 150.25);
updateStockPrice('GOOGL', 2800.75);
```

Explanation:

- o The `stockPriceUpdate` event is emitted when the stock price changes.
- o All listeners that are interested in this event will be notified, allowing the application to update the stock ticker in real-time.

Benefits of Event-Driven Programming with EventEmitters in Real-Time Apps

1. **Efficient Handling of Concurrent Tasks**: By using EventEmitters, Node.js can handle many tasks concurrently without blocking the main thread. This is especially important in real-time applications that require the server to respond to numerous simultaneous events, such as user input or external data changes.

2. **Scalability**: Event-driven systems can scale more easily because they're based on lightweight event loops and don't require the creation of multiple threads. This makes them more efficient in high-concurrency scenarios, such as chat applications or live notifications.

3. **Separation of Concerns**: Event-driven programming allows for cleaner, more modular code. Different parts of your application can listen for specific events and handle them independently without interfering with other parts of the system. For example, the frontend of a chat app may listen for new messages while the backend handles user authentication.

Summary

- **EventEmitters** in Node.js allow you to create custom events and listeners, enabling your application to react to events in an asynchronous and non-blocking way.

- **Event-driven programming** is a core part of Node.js, allowing you to handle many tasks simultaneously and efficiently.

- **Real-time applications** such as chat systems, notifications, and data updates can benefit from EventEmitters, as they provide an easy and scalable way to broadcast changes to clients as soon as they occur.

CHAPTER 8

REAL-TIME DATA PROCESSING WITH NODE.JS

In this chapter, we'll explore **real-time data processing** with Node.js. Real-time data processing is a critical component of many modern applications, such as live data feeds, video streaming, IoT (Internet of Things) systems, and financial applications. Node.js's built-in support for **streams** makes it an ideal platform for processing large data sets efficiently in real time.

Introduction to Streams

A **stream** is an abstract interface for working with data that comes in chunks, rather than all at once. This is especially useful when working with large amounts of data or when the data is continuously generated, such as in real-time applications.

Node.js has four core types of streams:

1. **Readable Streams**: Streams that allow you to read data from a source (e.g., reading data from a file or receiving data from a network).

2. **Writable Streams**: Streams that allow you to write data to a destination (e.g., writing to a file or sending data over a network).

3. **Duplex Streams**: Streams that are both readable and writable (e.g., network sockets).

4. **Transform Streams**: A special type of duplex stream where the output is a transformation of the input (e.g., compressing or encrypting data as it's read and written).

Node.js uses streams to handle I/O operations efficiently by processing data in **chunks** instead of loading everything into memory at once. This allows for **non-blocking I/O**, making it suitable for high-performance, real-time applications.

Real-Time Data Streams: Concepts and Examples

Real-time data streams are used in applications where data is continuously generated or updated, and the system needs to process and respond to it as soon as it arrives. Common real-time data stream examples include:

1. **WebSockets for Real-Time Messaging**: Messages are sent and received continuously over a WebSocket connection.

2. **Sensor Data from IoT Devices**: Data is streamed from sensors and processed in real time (e.g., temperature readings, motion detection).

3. **Stock Market Tickers**: Real-time price updates are streamed and displayed to users.

4. **Video and Audio Streaming**: Data is streamed from a server to a client without waiting for the entire file to load.

Let's walk through an example where we simulate a real-time data stream, such as a stream of stock prices.

Example: Stock Price Stream

```javascript
const { Readable } = require('stream');

// Simulate a stream of stock prices (every 1
second)
class StockPriceStream extends Readable {
  constructor(options) {
    super(options);
    this.prices = [100, 101, 102, 101, 103, 104];
    this.index = 0;
  }

  // Implement the _read method to push data into
the stream
  _read() {
    if (this.index < this.prices.length) {
      // Push the next stock price to the stream
```

```
this.push(this.prices[this.index].toString());
    this.index++;
  } else {
    // No more data, signal the end of the
stream
    this.push(null);
  }
 }
}


// Create a stock price stream and pipe it to
process.stdout
const stockStream = new StockPriceStream();

stockStream.on('data', (chunk) => {
  console.log(`New stock price: $${chunk}`);
});

stockStream.on('end', () => {
  console.log('Stream ended');
});
```

Explanation:

- **Readable stream**: We create a custom readable stream using the Readable class from the stream module. This class requires you to implement the _read() method, which is called to fetch new chunks of data.

- **Simulated stock prices**: We simulate stock prices in an array. Each time the _read() method is called, it pushes the next price to the stream. Once all prices are emitted, the stream ends.
- **data event**: We listen for the data event to print the stock prices to the console as they come in.
- **end event**: Once all data has been pushed, the end event is triggered.

Output:

pgsql

```
New stock price: $100
New stock price: $101
New stock price: $102
New stock price: $101
New stock price: $103
New stock price: $104
Stream ended
```

This is a simple example of a real-time data stream where stock prices are pushed to the console every second. In a real-world scenario, data might come from an external source (e.g., an API or WebSocket), and the data stream would need to handle large volumes of data continuously.

Processing Large Data Sets in Real-Time

One of the key advantages of using streams in Node.js is that they allow you to process large data sets without loading the entire data set into memory. This is particularly useful for real-time applications that deal with large amounts of data, such as:

- **Processing large log files**
- **Handling video or audio data streams**
- **Processing large JSON data from APIs**

Let's look at how you can use Node.js streams to process large files, such as reading a large log file in real time and processing its content.

Example: Real-Time Log File Processing

javascript

```javascript
const fs = require('fs');
const readline = require('readline');

// Create a readable stream from a large log file
const logStream = fs.createReadStream('large-log-file.txt', 'utf8');

// Create an interface to process the log file
line by line
const rl = readline.createInterface({
```

```
    input: logStream,
    output: process.stdout,
    terminal: false
});


rl.on('line', (line) => {
  // Process each line of the log file as it is
read
    console.log(`Processing log line: ${line}`);
});


rl.on('close', () => {
    console.log('Finished processing log file');
});
```

Explanation:

- **fs.createReadStream()**: We create a readable stream from a log file. The file is read in chunks, so we never load the entire file into memory.
- **readline module**: This module allows you to process the file line by line as it is read from the stream. This is useful when dealing with large files where processing each line individually is necessary.
- **line event**: For each line in the log file, the line event is triggered, and we can process that line (e.g., log it to the console or perform some analysis).

This approach allows us to handle large files efficiently in real time without running into memory issues.

Real-Time Data Processing in More Complex Scenarios

1. **Transform Streams**: You can create **transform streams** to modify data as it is read from a source and written to a destination. For example, you might want to compress or encrypt data on the fly while it is being streamed.

   Example: Data Compression Stream:

   javascript

   ```javascript
   const zlib = require('zlib');
   const fs = require('fs');

   const             readStream             =
   fs.createReadStream('large-file.txt');
   const             writeStream            =
   fs.createWriteStream('large-
   file.txt.gz');

   const gzip = zlib.createGzip(); // Create
   a gzip stream to compress data

   readStream
       .pipe(gzip)       // Pass the data through
   the gzip transform stream
   ```

87

```
.pipe(writeStream);      //   Write   the
compressed data to a new file
```

In this example, we read a large text file and compress it using the zlib module's createGzip() method, which is a transform stream. The data is compressed as it is read and written to the output file in real time.

2. **Processing Real-Time Sensor Data**: Consider an IoT system that collects data from multiple sensors, such as temperature or humidity. Using Node.js streams, you can process this sensor data in real time as it is received.

   Example: Real-Time Sensor Data Stream:

```javascript

const { Readable } = require('stream');

// Simulating a stream of sensor data
(temperature readings)
class SensorDataStream extends Readable {
  constructor(options) {
    super(options);
    this.data = [22.5, 23.1, 22.8, 23.3,
22.9]; // Temperature readings
    this.index = 0;
  }
```

```
_read() {
  if (this.index < this.data.length) {

this.push(this.data[this.index].toString(
));
    this.index++;
  } else {
    this.push(null); // End the stream
  }
 }
}


const          sensorStream      =        new
SensorDataStream();


sensorStream.on('data', (temp) => {
  console.log(`Sensor                reading:
${temp}°C`);
});
```

Explanation:

- o The `SensorDataStream` class simulates a stream of temperature data, which could come from actual sensors in a real-world application.
- o Each temperature reading is pushed to the stream, and when the data is received by the listener, it's processed (in this case, printed to the console).

Summary

- **Streams** in Node.js allow you to process data in **chunks**, making it ideal for real-time data processing. Streams handle large volumes of data efficiently by not loading everything into memory at once.
- **Readable Streams** are used to read data from sources (e.g., files, network connections), while **Writable Streams** allow you to send data to destinations.
- **Transform Streams** are useful for modifying data on the fly, such as compressing or encrypting data.
- Real-time applications, such as **sensor data streaming**, **log file processing**, and **real-time data feeds**, can benefit from Node.js's stream capabilities to handle continuous data efficiently.

By leveraging streams, you can build high-performance, real-time data processing applications that can scale to handle large data sets without running into memory or performance issues.

CHAPTER 9

ASYNCHRONOUS PROGRAMMING WITH PROMISES AND ASYNC/AWAIT

In this chapter, we will explore how **asynchronous programming** works in JavaScript, particularly in Node.js, and how you can handle asynchronous code more effectively using **Promises** and the **async/await** syntax. These tools allow for cleaner, more readable code while avoiding the pitfalls of traditional callback-based asynchronous programming.

Understanding Callbacks and Avoiding Callback Hell

Callbacks are one of the most common ways to handle asynchronous operations in JavaScript. A callback is a function that is passed into another function as an argument and is executed once the operation completes.

Here's a basic example of using a callback to handle asynchronous code:

```javascript
const fs = require('fs');
```

```
fs.readFile('file.txt', 'utf8', (err, data) => {
  if (err) {
    console.error('Error reading file:', err);
  } else {
    console.log('File content:', data);
  }
});
```

Callback Hell (also known as "Pyramid of Doom") occurs when you have nested callbacks within callbacks, leading to unreadable, difficult-to-maintain code. This happens when multiple asynchronous operations depend on each other, and each one requires a callback.

Here's an example of **callback hell**:

```
javascript

doSomething((err, result1) => {
  if (err) {
    console.error(err);
  } else {
    doSomethingElse(result1, (err, result2) => {
      if (err) {
        console.error(err);
      } else {
        doAnotherThing(result2,  (err,  result3)
=> {
```

```
        if (err) {
          console.error(err);
        } else {
          console.log('Final         result:',
result3);
        }
      });
    }
  });
  }
});
```

As you can see, the code becomes difficult to manage as you add more asynchronous operations. The nested structure makes it hard to track which operation is executing and how errors are handled.

Using Promises for Cleaner Code

Promises provide a way to avoid callback hell by allowing you to work with asynchronous code in a more linear, readable manner. A **Promise** represents a value that will be available in the future and provides a way to handle asynchronous results (or errors) using .then() and .catch() methods.

Here's how to use a **Promise** for cleaner asynchronous code:

```
javascript
```

```
const fs = require('fs');
```

```
function readFile(filePath) {
  return new Promise((resolve, reject) => {
    fs.readFile(filePath, 'utf8', (err, data) =>
{
      if (err) {
        reject(err);
      } else {
        resolve(data);
      }
    });
  });
}

readFile('file.txt')
  .then(data => {
    console.log('File content:', data);
  })
  .catch(err => {
    console.error('Error reading file:', err);
  });
```

Explanation:

- We wrap the `fs.readFile` operation in a **Promise**. The `resolve` function is called when the operation completes successfully, and the `reject` function is called if an error occurs.

- **then()** is used to handle the result when the promise is fulfilled.
- **catch()** is used to handle errors if the promise is rejected.

Advantages of Promises:

- They help avoid the nested structure of callback hell.
- They make it easier to chain multiple asynchronous operations in a more readable way.
- They provide a better way to handle errors in asynchronous code by centralizing error handling using `.catch()`.

Chaining Promises: Promises allow you to chain multiple operations together, making your code more readable and sequential:

```javascript
readFile('file.txt')
  .then(data => {
    console.log('File content:', data);
    return readFile('anotherFile.txt');    // Chain another operation
  })
  .then(data => {
    console.log('Another file content:', data);
```

```
})
.catch(err => {
  console.error('Error:', err);
});
```

In this example, after the first file is read, we chain another file reading operation. Each subsequent `.then()` waits for the previous one to resolve before executing.

async/await Syntax for Better Asynchronous Handling

The **async/await** syntax is a modern way to write asynchronous code that is more synchronous in appearance. It is built on top of Promises but makes working with asynchronous code even more readable by avoiding `.then()` chains.

- **async** is used to declare a function that will return a Promise.
- **await** is used inside an `async` function to pause execution until a Promise is resolved (or rejected), making it appear as though the code is synchronous.

Here's how you can rewrite the previous example using `async/await`:

javascript

```
const fs = require('fs');
```

```javascript
function readFile(filePath) {
  return new Promise((resolve, reject) => {
    fs.readFile(filePath, 'utf8', (err, data) =>
{
      if (err) {
        reject(err);
      } else {
        resolve(data);
      }
    });
  });
}

async function processFiles() {
  try {
    const data1 = await readFile('file.txt');
    console.log('File content:', data1);

    const           data2          =          await
readFile('anotherFile.txt');
    console.log('Another file content:', data2);
  } catch (err) {
    console.error('Error:', err);
  }
}

processFiles();
```

Explanation:

- **async function**: The `processFiles()` function is declared as `async`, which means it will always return a Promise, and we can use `await` inside it.
- **await expression**: Inside `processFiles()`, the `await` expression pauses the function execution until the `readFile()` Promise is resolved. It then continues to the next line of code after the Promise resolves.
- **Error Handling**: We use a `try...catch` block to handle errors. If any of the `await` calls reject the Promise, the error will be caught in the `catch` block.

Benefits of async/await:

- **More readable code**: The syntax is simpler and looks like synchronous code, making it easier to follow.
- **Better error handling**: Using `try...catch` for error handling is more straightforward than handling errors with `.catch()`.
- **Easier to maintain**: It avoids the complexity of nested callbacks and `.then()` chains, especially in larger applications.

Combining Promises with async/await

You can use `async/await` together with `Promise.all()` to run multiple asynchronous operations in parallel, which can improve performance when tasks don't depend on each other.

Here's an example:

javascript

```javascript
async function fetchData() {
    const          promise1          =
fetch('https://api.example.com/data1');
    const          promise2          =
fetch('https://api.example.com/data2');
    const          promise3          =
fetch('https://api.example.com/data3');

    try {
        const results = await Promise.all([promise1,
promise2, promise3]);
        const data1 = await results[0].json();
        const data2 = await results[1].json();
        const data3 = await results[2].json();
        console.log(data1, data2, data3);
    } catch (err) {
        console.error('Error fetching data:', err);
    }
}

fetchData();
```

Explanation:

- We create three separate fetch requests, which are wrapped in Promises.

99

- **Promise.all()** is used to wait for all the Promises to resolve. This allows us to run all the operations concurrently.
- After all Promises are resolved, we process the results.

This is an efficient way to handle multiple asynchronous operations that can run in parallel.

Summary

- **Callbacks** are the traditional way to handle asynchronous operations in JavaScript, but they can lead to **callback hell**, where nested callbacks make the code difficult to read and maintain.
- **Promises** offer a cleaner alternative, allowing you to chain asynchronous operations and handle errors more effectively.
- **async/await** provides an even more readable syntax for handling asynchronous operations by making asynchronous code look and behave more like synchronous code.
- Using **async/await** and **Promises** together makes your code more maintainable, readable, and easier to debug, especially when dealing with multiple asynchronous tasks.

CHAPTER 10

INTEGRATING WITH EXTERNAL APIS IN REAL-TIME APPS

In this chapter, we'll explore how to integrate external APIs into real-time applications using Node.js. External APIs are essential for fetching live data, such as weather updates, stock prices, social media feeds, and more. We'll cover how to **fetch data from third-party APIs**, how to **use WebSockets with external services**, and provide a **real-world example** of integrating weather data into your app.

Fetching Data from Third-Party APIs

Many real-time applications rely on external data sources, such as APIs, to provide information that is continuously updated. In Node.js, you can fetch data from third-party APIs using the built-in **http** or **https** modules, or more commonly, a popular HTTP client like **Axios** or **node-fetch**.

Let's first look at how to fetch data from a third-party API using **Axios**.

1. **Install Axios**:

```bash
npm install axios
```

2. Fetch Data from a Public API:

For this example, we'll use the **JSONPlaceholder API**, which is a free fake online REST API that you can use for testing and prototyping. We'll fetch user data from the API.

```javascript
const axios = require('axios');

async function fetchUserData() {
  try {
    const response = await axios.get('https://jsonplaceholder.typicode.com/users');
    console.log('User Data:', response.data);
  } catch (error) {
    console.error('Error fetching user data:', error);
  }
}

fetchUserData();
```

Explanation:

- We use **Axios** to send an HTTP GET request to the `https://jsonplaceholder.typicode.com/user s` endpoint.

- The `await` keyword ensures that the response is received before proceeding.

- The data returned by the API is logged to the console.

In a real-time application, this type of data fetching can be done repeatedly or triggered by certain events, such as user input or periodic updates.

Using WebSockets with External Services

In some cases, it's more efficient to use **WebSockets** for communication with external services, particularly when you want real-time data updates. WebSockets enable a persistent connection between your app and an external service, allowing data to be pushed to your app as soon as it changes.

Let's walk through how you can use WebSockets to connect to an external WebSocket service and receive real-time data.

Example: Integrating with a WebSocket-based API:

1. **Install ws** (if not already installed):

bash

```
npm install ws
```

2. Connecting to an External WebSocket Service:

For this example, let's assume we're integrating with a WebSocket service that provides real-time cryptocurrency prices.

```javascript
const WebSocket = require('ws');

// Connect to the WebSocket server (this is just
an example, use the correct URL for your service)
const ws = new WebSocket('wss://example-crypto-
websocket.com');

// When connected, subscribe to a specific
channel (e.g., Bitcoin price updates)
ws.on('open', () => {
  console.log('Connected to WebSocket server');
  ws.send(JSON.stringify({ type: 'subscribe',
channel: 'BTC/USD' }));
});

// When new data is received, handle it
ws.on('message', (data) => {
  const priceData = JSON.parse(data);
  console.log('Received    real-time    price:',
priceData);
});
```

```
// Handle WebSocket errors
ws.on('error', (error) => {
  console.error('WebSocket error:', error);
});

// Handle WebSocket closure
ws.on('close', () => {
  console.log('Disconnected    from    WebSocket
server');
});
```

Explanation:

- We connect to a WebSocket server using the `WebSocket` constructor.
- Once connected (`open` event), we send a message to subscribe to the `BTC/USD` price channel.
- As soon as new data is received (`message` event), it is parsed and logged.
- WebSocket connections are long-lived, meaning data will be pushed to your app in real-time.

Using WebSockets in this way enables real-time updates for things like stock prices, weather updates, or live scores in sports apps.

Real-World Example: Integrating Weather Data into Your App

Let's build a real-world example where we integrate **weather data** from an external API (OpenWeatherMap) into a real-time Node.js application. We'll use **Axios** to fetch weather data and **WebSockets** to display updates in real time.

1. **Set Up the Project**:
   - Install necessary dependencies:

bash

npm install axios ws

2. **Sign up for OpenWeatherMap API**:
   - Create an account on OpenWeatherMap and get an **API key**.
3. **Fetch Weather Data from OpenWeatherMap**:

Here's a simple application where we fetch weather data for a city (e.g., London) every 10 seconds and broadcast it to connected WebSocket clients.

javascript

```
const axios = require('axios');
const WebSocket = require('ws');

const API_KEY = 'your_openweathermap_api_key';
```

```
const CITY = 'London';
const           WEATHER_API_URL            =
`http://api.openweathermap.org/data/2.5/weather
?q=${CITY}&appid=${API_KEY}&units=metric`;

// Set up WebSocket server
const wss = new WebSocket.Server({ port: 8080 });

// When a client connects, send them a welcome
message
wss.on('connection', (ws) => {
  console.log('New client connected');
  ws.send('Welcome    to    the    Weather    WebSocket
Server!');
});

// Function to fetch weather data and broadcast
it to all connected clients
async function fetchWeatherData() {
  try {
    const       response       =       await
axios.get(WEATHER_API_URL);
    const weatherData = {
      city: CITY,
      temperature: response.data.main.temp,
      description:
response.data.weather[0].description,
    };
    console.log('Weather data:', weatherData);
```

```
    // Broadcast the weather data to all
connected WebSocket clients
    wss.clients.forEach(client => {
        if (client.readyState === WebSocket.OPEN)
{

client.send(JSON.stringify(weatherData));
        }
    });
  } catch (error) {
    console.error('Error    fetching    weather
data:', error);
  }
}


// Fetch weather data every 10 seconds and
broadcast
setInterval(fetchWeatherData, 10000); // Fetch
every 10 seconds
```

Explanation:

- **OpenWeatherMap API**: We use Axios to fetch the current weather for London. The data includes the temperature and weather description.
- **WebSocket Server**: A WebSocket server is set up on port 8080. When a client connects, it sends a welcome message.

- **Broadcasting Data**: The weather data is fetched every 10 seconds and broadcast to all connected WebSocket clients using `wss.clients.forEach`.

- **Real-time Updates**: Clients will receive the latest weather data in real time without needing to refresh their page.

4. **Setting Up the Frontend (Client)**:

Now let's create a simple HTML page where users can see the real-time weather updates.

```html
html

<!DOCTYPE html>
<html lang="en">
<head>
  <meta charset="UTF-8">
  <title>Real-Time Weather</title>
</head>
<body>
  <h1>Weather Updates</h1>
  <div id="weather"></div>

  <script>
    const          ws          =          new
WebSocket('ws://localhost:8080');

    ws.onopen = () => {
```

109

```
        console.log('Connected    to    the    weather
WebSocket server');
    };

    ws.onmessage = (event) => {
        const              weatherData              =
JSON.parse(event.data);

document.getElementById('weather').innerHTML = `
            <p>City: ${weatherData.city}</p>
            <p>Temperature:
${weatherData.temperature} °C</p>
            <p>Description:
${weatherData.description}</p>
        `;
    };

    ws.onerror = (error) => {
        console.error('WebSocket error:', error);
    };

    ws.onclose = () => {
        console.log('Disconnected    from    the
WebSocket server');
    };
  </script>
</body>
</html>
```

Explanation:

- The client connects to the WebSocket server on `localhost:8080`.

- Every time a message is received (`onmessage`), the weather data is displayed in the `#weather` div.

- The WebSocket connection is kept open to receive real-time weather updates as they are broadcasted by the server.

Summary

- **Fetching Data from Third-Party APIs**: We used **Axios** to fetch data from external APIs (such as OpenWeatherMap) and integrate it into our Node.js app. This allows real-time apps to access external data like weather, stock prices, or social media updates.

- **WebSockets with External Services**: We used **WebSockets** to receive and broadcast real-time data, such as live weather updates, to multiple clients simultaneously.

- **Real-World Example**: We built a real-time weather application that fetches data from an external weather API and sends updates to connected clients using WebSockets.

By integrating external APIs and WebSockets, you can build powerful real-time applications that provide users with up-to-date information, creating a more dynamic and engaging experience.

CHAPTER 11

DATA STORAGE FOR REAL-TIME APPLICATIONS

In real-time applications, the way data is stored and retrieved is crucial for performance and scalability. In this chapter, we'll explore how to choose the right type of database for your application and how to use **MongoDB** for real-time data storage. We'll also cover how to set up **real-time database listeners** to ensure that your application can respond to changes in the data as they happen.

Choosing the Right Database: SQL vs NoSQL

When choosing a database for a real-time application, the choice between **SQL (relational)** and **NoSQL (non-relational)** databases can significantly affect performance and scalability. Both types of databases have their strengths, and the decision often depends on the specific requirements of your app.

1. **SQL Databases** (Relational):
   - **Examples**: MySQL, PostgreSQL, SQLite.
   - **Structure**: SQL databases are structured around tables and rows, and they use SQL (Structured

Query Language) for data retrieval and manipulation.

o **Use Cases**: Best for applications that require complex queries, transactions, and data integrity.

o **ACID Compliance**: SQL databases generally offer strong consistency, supporting **ACID** (Atomicity, Consistency, Isolation, Durability) properties, which ensures reliable transactions.

o **Limitations**: They might not scale as efficiently as NoSQL databases in distributed systems or handle unstructured or semi-structured data well.

2. **NoSQL Databases** (Non-relational):

o **Examples**: MongoDB, CouchDB, Cassandra, Redis.

o **Structure**: NoSQL databases store data in a variety of formats such as key-value pairs, documents, graphs, or wide-column stores. They are designed to be flexible and scalable.

o **Use Cases**: Ideal for real-time apps with dynamic data models, massive scale, and low-latency requirements, such as chat apps, recommendation engines, and sensor data streams.

o **Eventual Consistency**: NoSQL databases often focus on high availability and partition tolerance (as per the **CAP Theorem**) but may offer eventual consistency over strict consistency.

For Real-Time Applications:

- **NoSQL** databases like MongoDB are often better suited for real-time apps due to their ability to handle large volumes of unstructured or semi-structured data and their horizontal scalability. They can efficiently store data in JSON-like documents, which is perfect for handling dynamic, real-time data.

Using MongoDB for Real-Time Data Storage

MongoDB is one of the most popular NoSQL databases and is particularly well-suited for real-time applications. It is a document-oriented database, which stores data in flexible **BSON (Binary JSON)** format, making it easy to store dynamic, unstructured data. MongoDB's ability to scale horizontally and handle large amounts of data with low-latency operations makes it an excellent choice for real-time systems.

1. **Install MongoDB**:
   - You can set up MongoDB either locally or use a cloud service like **MongoDB Atlas**.
   - To install MongoDB locally, follow the instructions on MongoDB's official website.
2. **Install MongoDB Node.js Driver**:
   - To interact with MongoDB from a Node.js application, you need the official MongoDB

Node.js driver or **Mongoose** (an ODM for MongoDB).

Install the MongoDB Node.js driver:

bash

```
npm install mongodb
```

Or install Mongoose (if you prefer using an ODM):

bash

```
npm install mongoose
```

3. **Connecting to MongoDB**: Here's how you connect to a MongoDB database and perform some basic operations using the MongoDB Node.js driver.

javascript

```
const { MongoClient } = require('mongodb');

// Connection URI and Database Name
const uri = 'mongodb://localhost:27017';
const dbName = 'realTimeApp';

// Create a new MongoClient
```

```javascript
const client = new MongoClient(uri, {
useNewUrlParser: true, useUnifiedTopology: true
});

async function main() {
  try {
    // Connect to MongoDB
    await client.connect();

    // Get the database and collection
    const db = client.db(dbName);
    const collection =
db.collection('messages');

    // Insert a new message
    const result = await collection.insertOne({
      username: 'JohnDoe',
      message: 'Hello, World!',
      timestamp: new Date(),
    });
    console.log('Message inserted with _id:',
result.insertedId);

    // Find all messages
    const messages = await
collection.find({}).toArray();
    console.log('Messages:', messages);

  } finally {
```

```
    // Close the connection
    await client.close();
  }
}


main().catch(console.error);
```

Explanation:

- **MongoClient** is used to connect to the MongoDB server. The connection string (uri) points to the local MongoDB instance, and dbName refers to the database.

- **insertOne()** inserts a new message into the messages collection.

- **find()** retrieves all messages from the messages collection.

Setting Up Real-Time Database Listeners

In real-time applications, you may need to listen for changes in the database, such as when a new message is inserted or when existing data is updated. MongoDB provides **Change Streams** to handle this.

Change Streams allow you to watch for changes to documents in a collection in real time, which is especially useful for applications like chat apps, live notifications, and real-time dashboards.

117

1. **Setting up Change Streams with MongoDB**:

```javascript
const { MongoClient } = require('mongodb');

// Connection URI and Database Name
const uri = 'mongodb://localhost:27017';
const dbName = 'realTimeApp';

// Create a new MongoClient
const client = new MongoClient(uri, {
useNewUrlParser: true, useUnifiedTopology: true
});

async function watchChanges() {
  try {
    // Connect to MongoDB
    await client.connect();

    // Get the database and collection
    const db = client.db(dbName);
    const collection =
db.collection('messages');

    // Watch for changes to the collection (using
Change Streams)
    const changeStream = collection.watch();
```

```
    console.log('Watching  for  changes  in  the
"messages" collection...');

    // Listen for changes and handle them in real
time
    changeStream.on('change', (change) => {
        console.log('Change detected:', change);
        // For example, broadcasting the change to
clients using WebSockets
    });

  } catch (err) {
    console.error('Error    watching    changes:',
err);
  }
}

watchChanges().catch(console.error);
```

Explanation:

- **watch()** on a collection creates a Change Stream that watches for insertions, updates, deletions, etc.
- **on('change')** listens for changes in the collection. When a change is detected, the provided callback function is executed, where you can process or broadcast the change to clients in real time.

119

Broadcasting Changes to Clients in Real Time

In a real-time chat app, for example, when a new message is added to the database, you might want to broadcast this message to all connected WebSocket clients. Here's how you can integrate the change stream with **WebSocket**:

javascript

```javascript
const WebSocket = require('ws');
const { MongoClient } = require('mongodb');

const uri = 'mongodb://localhost:27017';
const dbName = 'realTimeApp';
const wss = new WebSocket.Server({ port: 8080 });

// WebSocket clients array
let clients = [];

wss.on('connection', (ws) => {
  console.log('New WebSocket client connected');
  clients.push(ws);

  // Handle disconnections
  ws.on('close', () => {
    clients = clients.filter(client => client !==
ws);
  });
});
```

```
async function watchChanges() {
  const client = new MongoClient(uri, {
useNewUrlParser: true, useUnifiedTopology: true
});

  try {
    await client.connect();
    const db = client.db(dbName);
    const                collection              =
db.collection('messages');
    const changeStream = collection.watch();

    console.log('Watching for changes in the
"messages" collection...');

    changeStream.on('change', (change) => {
      console.log('Change detected:', change);

      // Broadcast the change (new message) to
all WebSocket clients
      clients.forEach(client => {
        if        (client.readyState       ===
WebSocket.OPEN) {

client.send(JSON.stringify(change.fullDocument)
); // Send the updated message
        }
      });
```

```
    });
  } catch (err) {
    console.error('Error   watching   changes:',
err);
  }
}


watchChanges().catch(console.error);
```

Explanation:

- When a WebSocket client connects, the server adds them to the `clients` array.
- The **Change Stream** watches for changes in the `messages` collection.
- When a new message is inserted, the server broadcasts the change to all connected clients in real time.

Summary

- **Choosing the Right Database**: SQL databases work well for structured data and complex queries, while NoSQL databases like **MongoDB** excel in real-time applications with large, dynamic, and unstructured data.
- **Using MongoDB for Real-Time Data Storage**: MongoDB's flexible document model and horizontal scalability make it ideal for handling real-time data, such as chat messages, sensor data, or user activity.

- **Setting Up Real-Time Database Listeners**: MongoDB's **Change Streams** allow you to listen for real-time changes in the database and broadcast these changes to clients using technologies like **WebSockets**.

With MongoDB's real-time capabilities, you can easily build scalable, real-time applications that provide immediate feedback to users based on changes in the underlying data.

CHAPTER 12

HANDLING REAL-TIME NOTIFICATIONS

Real-time notifications are a critical feature in modern web and mobile applications. They allow applications to notify users instantly about important events or updates, such as new messages, mentions, or status changes. In this chapter, we'll explore two main technologies for real-time notifications—**Push Notifications** and **WebSockets**—and we'll also discuss how to implement notifications using services like **Firebase**.

Push Notifications vs. WebSockets

Both **Push Notifications** and **WebSockets** enable real-time communication, but they have different use cases and implementations. Let's compare both:

1. **Push Notifications**:
    o **Definition**: Push notifications are messages that are sent from a server to a client (usually a mobile app or a web browser) even when the client is not actively using the app.
    o **How it Works**: The server sends a message through a push service (e.g., Firebase Cloud

Messaging, Apple Push Notification Service), and the notification is delivered to the client. Push notifications are typically used for apps where users don't need to be actively connected at all times (e.g., email notifications, news alerts).

- o **Advantages**:
  - Works when the app is in the background or not open.
  - Less resource-intensive on the client-side (compared to WebSockets).
  - Can be used across different platforms (mobile and web).
- o **Disadvantages**:
  - Requires integration with a third-party service (e.g., Firebase or APNs).
  - Some platforms (e.g., iOS) may have restrictions on the frequency of push notifications.

2. **WebSockets**:
   - o **Definition**: WebSockets provide a persistent, bidirectional connection between the client and server, allowing data to be transmitted instantly in real time.
   - o **How it Works**: When the client connects to the server via WebSocket, the connection remains open, and both the client and server can send

125

messages to each other at any time. WebSockets are ideal for chat applications, live notifications, and real-time data feeds.

- o **Advantages**:
  - Real-time, low-latency communication.
  - Ideal for use cases where continuous interaction between client and server is needed.
  - Direct communication, no need for third-party services.
- o **Disadvantages**:
  - Requires the client to be actively connected.
  - Can consume more resources (e.g., on mobile devices) because of the persistent connection.
  - May not be suitable for apps that need notifications when the app is closed or not in use.

Implementing Real-Time Notifications

Real-time notifications are most commonly used in applications like messaging apps, social media platforms, and collaborative tools. Let's walk through how to implement **real-time notifications** using **WebSockets** and **Push Notifications**.

1. Implementing WebSocket-Based Real-Time Notifications

In a real-time app, notifications can be triggered based on specific events (e.g., when a new message arrives or a user gets a mention). Let's create a simple WebSocket server where notifications are sent to users in real time when a new message is posted.

Example: Real-Time Chat Notifications with WebSockets

javascript

```javascript
const WebSocket = require('ws');

// Set up the WebSocket server
const wss = new WebSocket.Server({ port: 8080 });

// Store connected clients
let clients = [];

wss.on('connection', (ws) => {
  console.log('New client connected');
  clients.push(ws);

  // Handle new messages and broadcast them
  ws.on('message', (message) => {
    console.log('Received message:', message);

    // Broadcast the message to all other clients
```

127

```
clients.forEach(client => {
    if (client !== ws && client.readyState ===
WebSocket.OPEN) {
        client.send(`New message: ${message}`);
    }
  });
});


// Handle disconnections
ws.on('close', () => {
    clients = clients.filter(client => client !==
ws);
    console.log('A client disconnected');
  });
});


console.log('WebSocket    server    running    at
ws://localhost:8080');
```

Explanation:

- **WebSocket Server**: We create a WebSocket server using
  the ws module. Each time a new client connects, they are
  added to the clients array.
- **Message Broadcasting**: When a client sends a message,
  the server broadcasts the message to all other connected
  clients.
- **Real-Time Notifications**: As soon as a new message is
  posted, all clients receive a notification in real time.

2. Implementing Push Notifications

While WebSockets are great for real-time interactions while the user is active in the app, **Push Notifications** are more suited for notifying users when they are not actively using the app. For this, we'll use **Firebase Cloud Messaging (FCM)** to send push notifications to both web and mobile clients.

Firebase Cloud Messaging (FCM) allows you to send notifications to your app's users on Android, iOS, or the web. Let's see how to implement push notifications using Firebase.

Step-by-Step Guide: Implementing Push Notifications with Firebase

1. **Set up Firebase**:
   o   Go to the Firebase Console.
   o   Create a new project.
   o   Add Firebase to your web or mobile app. You'll need the **Firebase SDK** for your platform (Web, iOS, or Android).
2. **Install Firebase SDK** (for Node.js): To send push notifications from your Node.js server, install Firebase Admin SDK.

bash

```
npm install firebase-admin
```

3. **Initialize Firebase in Your Node.js App**:

```javascript
const admin = require('firebase-admin');

// Initialize Firebase Admin SDK
admin.initializeApp({
  credential:
admin.credential.applicationDefault(),
  databaseURL:          'https://your-database-
name.firebaseio.com',
});

const messaging = admin.messaging();

// Send a push notification
async    function    sendPushNotification(token,
title, body) {
  const message = {
    notification: {
      title: title,
      body: body,
    },
    token: token, // The device token of the
recipient
  };

  try {
```

```
    const          response          =          await
messaging.send(message);
    console.log('Push       notification       sent
successfully:', response);
  } catch (error) {
    console.error('Error       sending       push
notification:', error);
  }
}


// Example usage: sending a push notification
const deviceToken = 'your-device-token';
sendPushNotification(deviceToken, 'New Message',
'You have received a new message!');
```

Explanation:

- **Firebase Admin SDK**: We initialize the Firebase Admin SDK with credentials, which allows the server to send notifications to users.
- **sendPushNotification()**: This function sends a push notification to a specific device using the device's registration token.
- **Notification Format**: We define the notification's title and body, which will be displayed on the user's device.

3. Using Firebase for Web Push Notifications

To send push notifications to web clients, you'll need to integrate Firebase with your frontend. Here's a simplified version of how to set up push notifications in a web application.

1. **Install Firebase Web SDK**:

bash

```
npm install firebase
```

2. **Frontend: Request Permission and Receive Push Notifications**:

javascript

```
import firebase from 'firebase/app';
import 'firebase/messaging';

// Initialize Firebase
firebase.initializeApp({
  apiKey: 'your-api-key',
  authDomain: 'your-project-id.firebaseapp.com',
  projectId: 'your-project-id',
  messagingSenderId: 'your-sender-id',
  appId: 'your-app-id',
});
```

```
// Get Firebase Messaging instance
const messaging = firebase.messaging();

// Request permission to show notifications
async function requestNotificationPermission() {
  try {
    await Notification.requestPermission();
    const token = await messaging.getToken();
    console.log('Firebase token:', token);

    // Send token to your server to send push
notifications
  } catch (error) {
    console.error('Error requesting notification
permission:', error);
  }
}

// Handle incoming messages when app is in the
foreground
messaging.onMessage((payload) => {
  console.log('Message received:', payload);
  // Show notification or update the UI
accordingly
});
```

Explanation:

- **Request Permission**: We ask the user for permission to show notifications via the browser.

- **Get Device Token**: If permission is granted, we retrieve the device token, which is unique to the device or browser and used for sending targeted notifications.
- **Foreground Notifications**: We listen for incoming notifications while the app is in the foreground using `onMessage()`.

Summary

- **Push Notifications** and **WebSockets** are both used to deliver real-time notifications, but they serve different purposes:
    o **Push Notifications** are ideal for notifying users when they are not actively using the app (e.g., mobile and web notifications).
    o **WebSockets** provide real-time communication between the client and server while the app is open and active.
- **Firebase Cloud Messaging (FCM)** is a powerful service for sending push notifications to mobile and web clients, enabling cross-platform notification delivery.
- **Real-Time Notifications** can be implemented using **WebSockets** for active communication or **Push Notifications** for notifying users in the background. Both methods can be integrated with services like Firebase to handle the notification lifecycle effectively.

By integrating these methods into your application, you can keep your users informed in real time, improving user engagement and experience.

CHAPTER 13

SCALING NODE.JS FOR REAL-TIME APPLICATIONS

Scaling is a crucial aspect of building real-time applications that need to handle large numbers of simultaneous connections, requests, and data streams. Node.js, being a single-threaded platform, introduces unique challenges and opportunities for scaling. In this chapter, we will explore the **scalability challenges** in Node.js, how to achieve **horizontal scaling** using **Node.js clusters**, and discuss **load balancing** and **sharding strategies** to ensure that your application can scale efficiently.

Understanding Scalability Challenges

Node.js is known for its ability to handle a large number of simultaneous connections due to its **event-driven, non-blocking I/O model**. However, this single-threaded nature presents certain challenges when it comes to scaling applications across multiple CPU cores and handling high loads effectively.

1. **Single-Threaded Event Loop**: Node.js uses a single-threaded event loop to handle all incoming requests. While this design is highly efficient for I/O-bound operations, it can be a limitation for CPU-

136

bound tasks, such as complex computations or processing large datasets. If one request takes too long, it can block the entire event loop, causing delays for all incoming requests.

2. **Limited Use of Multi-Core Systems**: Most modern servers have multi-core processors. However, Node.js, by default, runs on a single core, meaning that it doesn't automatically take advantage of multiple cores. This can limit scalability when trying to handle large numbers of requests or connections.

3. **Memory and Resource Management**: As your application scales, the amount of data being processed can grow significantly. Managing memory usage and ensuring that resources are allocated efficiently becomes crucial, especially when dealing with large amounts of data in real-time applications.

Horizontal Scaling with Node.js Clusters

One of the most common ways to scale a Node.js application is by using **horizontal scaling**, where multiple instances of your application run across multiple CPU cores. Node.js has a built-in **cluster** module that helps you achieve this by creating multiple worker processes, each of which can handle incoming requests.

1. **Node.js Cluster Module**: The **cluster** module allows you to spawn multiple Node.js

worker processes that share the same server port. This approach enables your application to take full advantage of multi-core systems and handle more concurrent connections.

Example: Creating a Cluster with Node.js

```javascript
const cluster = require('cluster');
const http = require('http');
const os = require('os');

const numCPUs = os.cpus().length; // Number of
CPU cores on the machine

// If this process is the master, create worker
processes
if (cluster.isMaster) {
  console.log(`Master        ${process.pid}        is
running`);

  // Fork workers for each CPU core
  for (let i = 0; i < numCPUs; i++) {
    cluster.fork();
  }

  cluster.on('exit', (worker, code, signal) => {
```

```
    console.log(`Worker      ${worker.process.pid}
died`);
  });
} else {
  // Workers can share the same server port
  http.createServer((req, res) => {
    res.writeHead(200);
    res.end('Hello, world!\n');
  }).listen(8000);

  console.log(`Worker ${process.pid} started`);
}
```

Explanation:

- The master process creates worker processes using `cluster.fork()`. Each worker is responsible for handling HTTP requests.
- The workers share the same server port (8000) and process requests independently, allowing the application to handle more traffic by distributing the load.
- **os.cpus()** returns the number of CPU cores available on the machine, so we can scale the application based on the system's resources.

By using the cluster module, your application can scale to utilize multiple cores and handle more concurrent connections.

Load Balancing and Sharding Strategies

As your Node.js application grows, simply adding more worker processes may not be enough to scale effectively. You'll need to implement **load balancing** and **sharding strategies** to ensure that requests are distributed efficiently across servers, and data is partitioned to handle high loads.

1. **Load** **Balancing**:
   Load balancing is the process of distributing incoming network traffic across multiple servers to ensure that no single server is overwhelmed with requests. There are two main types of load balancing strategies:
   - o **Round-robin**: Requests are distributed evenly across all available servers.
   - o **Least connections**: New requests are directed to the server with the fewest active connections.
   - o **IP Hashing**: Requests from the same client IP are always directed to the same server.

   Example: Using NGINX for Load Balancing:

   One common approach to load balancing with Node.js applications is to use a reverse proxy like **NGINX**. NGINX can balance the traffic between multiple instances of your Node.js application running on different server processes or even on different machines.

Here's a basic example of an NGINX configuration for load balancing:

nginx

```
http {
  upstream node_app {
    server 127.0.0.1:3000;
    server 127.0.0.1:3001;
    server 127.0.0.1:3002;
  }

  server {
    listen 80;

    location / {
      proxy_pass http://node_app;
      proxy_http_version 1.1;
      proxy_set_header                Upgrade
$http_upgrade;
      proxy_set_header             Connection
'upgrade';
      proxy_set_header Host $host;
      proxy_cache_bypass $http_upgrade;
    }
  }
}
```

Explanation:

- o The **upstream** directive defines a pool of Node.js application instances running on different ports.
- o The **proxy_pass** directive tells NGINX to forward all incoming traffic to one of the servers in the upstream pool.
- o NGINX will handle load balancing and ensure that the requests are evenly distributed among the Node.js instances.

2. **Sharding**:

Sharding is a database architecture pattern that divides data across multiple databases or servers, each called a "shard." This allows you to scale your database horizontally and distribute the data more effectively.

- o **Horizontal Sharding**: Data is partitioned across multiple databases by distributing different ranges of data (e.g., user IDs or product categories) across different servers.
- o **Vertical Sharding**: Data is partitioned by types or models (e.g., users in one database, orders in another).

In the context of Node.js, you might use **sharding** to split the load of database operations across multiple instances of a database (e.g., MongoDB or MySQL).

Example: Sharding with MongoDB:

MongoDB supports sharding natively, and you can configure it to distribute your data across multiple shards for better scalability.

```javascript
const { MongoClient } = require('mongodb');

const client = new MongoClient('mongodb://localhost:27017', { useUnifiedTopology: true });

async function setupSharding() {
  try {
    await client.connect();
    const db = client.db('realTimeApp');

    // Enable sharding on a database
    await db.admin().command({ enableSharding: 'realTimeApp' });

    // Shard a collection (e.g., messages) by a field (e.g., user_id)
    await db.admin().command({
      shardCollection: 'realTimeApp.messages',
      key: { user_id: 1 }
    });
```

```
    console.log('Sharding          setup
complete');
  } catch (err) {
    console.error('Error     setting     up
sharding:', err);
  } finally {
    await client.close();
  }
}


setupSharding().catch(console.error);
```

Explanation:

- o **enableSharding**: This command enables sharding on the specified database (`realTimeApp`).
- o **shardCollection**: This command sets up sharding for a specific collection (in this case, the `messages` collection), partitioning the data based on the `user_id` field.

Sharding helps distribute the load and ensures that your database can scale horizontally as your application grows.

Summary

- • **Scalability Challenges** in Node.js stem from its single-threaded nature. To overcome this, we use **horizontal** scaling by creating multiple worker processes using the **cluster** module, which allows Node.js to fully utilize multi-core processors.

- **Load Balancing** is essential for distributing incoming traffic across multiple servers, ensuring that no single instance is overwhelmed. Tools like **NGINX** provide efficient load balancing strategies.

- **Sharding** is a database partitioning technique that distributes data across multiple databases or servers, allowing for horizontal scaling of the database. MongoDB, for example, offers native support for sharding.

By combining these strategies, you can scale your Node.js applications to handle increasing traffic and large amounts of real-time data, ensuring both high performance and availability.

CHAPTER 14

AUTHENTICATION AND SECURITY FOR REAL-TIME APPS

In real-time applications, ensuring the security and integrity of the data transmitted between the server and clients is crucial. In this chapter, we'll focus on securing **WebSocket connections**, using **JWT (JSON Web Tokens)** for **authentication**, and implementing **real-time session management** to address various security concerns.

Securing WebSocket Connections

WebSockets are inherently designed for low-latency, real-time communication, which makes them a great fit for real-time applications. However, WebSocket connections can also be vulnerable if not properly secured. Here's how you can secure WebSocket connections:

1. **Use Secure WebSockets (wss://)**: Just as with HTTPS for secure HTTP connections, you should use **wss://** instead of **ws://** to ensure that your WebSocket communication is encrypted. This prevents man-in-the-middle attacks, where an attacker intercepts or manipulates the data being sent between the client and the server.

To use `wss://`, you need to set up an **SSL/TLS** certificate for your server. This can be done using services like **Let's Encrypt** for free certificates, or by using a commercial SSL provider.

Example of using `wss://` with Node.js:

```javascript
const fs = require('fs');
const https = require('https');
const WebSocket = require('ws');

// SSL certificates
const serverOptions = {
  key: fs.readFileSync('path/to/your/ssl-key.pem'),
  cert: fs.readFileSync('path/to/your/ssl-cert.pem')
};

// Create HTTPS server
const server = https.createServer(serverOptions);

// Set up WebSocket server
const wss = new WebSocket.Server({ server });
```

```
wss.on('connection', (ws) => {
  console.log('Client          connected
securely');
  ws.on('message', (message) => {
    console.log('Received        message:',
message);
  });
});


server.listen(8080, () => {
  console.log('Secure   WebSocket   server
running at wss://localhost:8080');
});
```

2. **Authenticate WebSocket Connections**: WebSocket connections, by default, are anonymous. To ensure that only authenticated users can connect, you should implement authentication before upgrading the HTTP connection to WebSocket. This can be done via **HTTP headers** or **query parameters** passed during the WebSocket handshake.

Here's an example using **JWT** authentication to secure the WebSocket connection:

Frontend (Client-side):

```
javascript
```

```
const               token              =
localStorage.getItem('authToken');        //
Retrieve the JWT from localStorage

const          ws          =          new
WebSocket(`wss://localhost:8080?token=${t
oken}`);    // Pass the token as a query
parameter

ws.onopen = () => {
  console.log('Connected    to    WebSocket
server');
};

ws.onmessage = (event) => {
  console.log('Message          received:',
event.data);
};
```

Backend (Server-side with WebSocket Authentication):

```javascript
const WebSocket = require('ws');
const jwt = require('jsonwebtoken');

const               server              =
require('https').createServer({    /*    SSL
options */ });
```

```
const wss = new WebSocket.Server({ server
});

wss.on('connection', (ws, req) => {
  const                token                =
req.url.split('?token=')[1];  // Get token
from query parameters

  // Validate the token
  jwt.verify(token,      'your-secret-key',
(err, decoded) => {
    if (err) {
      ws.close();  // Close the connection
if the token is invalid
      console.log('Invalid token');
    } else {
      console.log('Authenticated   user:',
decoded.username);
    }
  });
});

server.listen(8080, () => {
  console.log('Secure   WebSocket   server
listening on wss://localhost:8080');
});
```

Explanation:

- o The client sends a **JWT token** in the query parameter when connecting to the WebSocket server.
- o The server **verifies the JWT** using the `jwt.verify()` method. If the token is valid, the WebSocket connection is allowed; otherwise, it is closed.

3. **WebSocket Authorization**: After authenticating the user, you may want to implement role-based authorization. This can be done by inspecting the user's roles or permissions within the JWT, and restricting access to certain WebSocket channels based on that information.

Authentication with JWT (JSON Web Tokens)

JWT (JSON Web Token) is a compact and self-contained way to securely transmit information between parties as a JSON object. It is widely used for authenticating users and ensuring secure communication in real-time apps.

1. **Generating a JWT**: The server generates a JWT when the user logs in, and the token is sent to the client for future requests.

```javascript
const jwt = require('jsonwebtoken');
```

```
function generateToken(user) {
  const payload = {
    username: user.username,
    role: user.role
  };

  // Generate a token with a secret key and
an expiration time of 1 hour
    return  jwt.sign(payload,  'your-secret-
key', { expiresIn: '1h' });
}

// Example usage
const  token  =  generateToken({  username:
'john_doe', role: 'admin' });
console.log('Generated JWT:', token);
```

Explanation:

- o The jwt.sign() method generates a token with a **payload** (e.g., user info and role) and signs it with a **secret key**.

- o The token is usually sent to the client as a response to a successful login request. The client stores it (e.g., in localStorage or sessionStorage for web apps, or AsyncStorage for mobile apps).

2. **Verifying the JWT**: On the server side, before performing sensitive operations (such as accessing protected WebSocket channels), the JWT is verified to ensure that the user is authenticated.

```javascript
const jwt = require('jsonwebtoken');

function verifyToken(token) {
  try {
    const decoded = jwt.verify(token, 'your-secret-key');
    console.log('Decoded token:', decoded);
    return decoded;
  } catch (err) {
    console.error('Token verification failed:', err);
    return null;
  }
}
```

Explanation:

o The jwt.verify() method is used to verify the token's authenticity. If the token is valid, it returns the decoded data (e.g., user info). If the token is invalid or expired, an error is thrown.

153

3. **Storing the JWT**: After a user logs in and receives a JWT, the token can be stored client-side (in **localStorage**, **sessionStorage**, or **cookies**) and sent along with future API requests or WebSocket connections to authenticate the user.

Real-Time Session Management and Security Concerns

Real-time applications often require managing sessions efficiently, particularly when the app has multiple concurrent users or when the user's status changes frequently. Here's how to manage sessions securely in real-time apps:

1. **Session Expiry**: JWT tokens usually have an **expiration time** set during creation (e.g., 1 hour). After this period, the user must log in again to get a new token. This helps protect against **stale sessions**.
   - For long-running sessions, consider implementing **refresh tokens** that allow users to obtain a new JWT without re-authenticating. The refresh token is stored securely and has a longer lifespan than the access token.
2. **Session Invalidation**: If a user logs out or their session is revoked (e.g., due to a password change or account suspension), the corresponding JWT should be invalidated. For added security:

- o Store the JWT in **secure storage** (e.g., **httpOnly cookies**) to prevent cross-site scripting (XSS) attacks.
- o Implement a **blacklist** of revoked tokens, though this adds complexity to session management.

3. **Preventing Cross-Site WebSocket Hijacking**: Just like traditional HTTP sessions, WebSocket sessions are susceptible to hijacking. To prevent this, ensure the WebSocket server:

- o Uses **wss://** (WebSocket Secure) to encrypt the communication.
- o Authenticates the user before establishing a connection using JWT, as discussed earlier.
- o Uses **origin checking** to ensure that WebSocket connections are only accepted from trusted origins (e.g., the same domain as your app).

4. **Rate Limiting and DoS Protection**: Implement **rate limiting** to prevent abuse and protect against **Denial of Service (DoS)** attacks:

- o Use libraries like **Express-rate-limit** or **rate-limiter-flexible** to limit the number of requests or WebSocket messages a user can make within a certain time period.
- o Combine this with user authentication (JWT) to ensure each client is identified and tracked correctly.

Summary

- **Securing WebSocket Connections**: Use **wss://** for secure WebSocket connections and authenticate clients before they connect using methods like **JWT**.

- **JWT Authentication**: JSON Web Tokens are used to securely transmit authentication data and ensure that only authenticated users can access sensitive data or perform protected actions.

- **Real-Time Session Management**: Manage sessions securely by setting token expiration times, invalidating tokens on logout, and using refresh tokens for long-lived sessions.

- **Security Concerns**: Protect WebSocket connections from hijacking, ensure secure storage of tokens, and implement measures like **rate limiting** to protect your application from abuse.

By implementing proper authentication, security, and session management, you can ensure that your real-time applications remain secure and provide a safe experience for users.

CHAPTER 15

REAL-TIME COLLABORATION: BUILDING A COLLABORATIVE APP

Real-time collaboration has become a key feature in many modern applications, ranging from document editors to design tools and team communication platforms. In this chapter, we will explore the concepts of **collaborative applications**, **real-time synchronization techniques**, and then walk through an example of building a **real-time document editor**.

Concepts of Collaborative Applications

Collaborative applications allow multiple users to work on the same data, document, or task at the same time. This could include editing a document, drawing on a shared canvas, or collaborating on a project. The core idea is to keep all users in sync, with their changes reflecting in real-time across different clients.

Key concepts include:

1. **Simultaneous Editing**: Multiple users should be able to edit the same document or project simultaneously, and their changes should be reflected instantly for everyone.

2. **Conflict Resolution**: In collaborative environments, there is always the potential for users to make conflicting changes. A robust conflict resolution strategy is necessary to ensure the data remains consistent.

3. **Live Updates**: Every change made by a user should be sent to the server, which will then broadcast the update to all other connected users.

4. **Presence Indicators**: Showing which users are currently viewing or editing the document is often an important part of collaborative tools.

5. **Optimistic Updates**: Often, when a user makes a change, the system updates the UI immediately to reflect the change, even before the server confirms the update. This provides a more responsive user experience.

Real-Time Synchronization Techniques

There are several approaches to synchronizing data in real-time collaborative applications. Here are some of the most common techniques:

1. **Operational Transformation (OT)**:
   - **Description**: This algorithm synchronizes operations across multiple clients by

transforming operations as they are applied. This ensures that operations are consistent even when they occur out of order or simultaneously. Google Docs is one of the most well-known examples of OT in action.

- o **How it Works**: When two users make changes to the same part of the document at the same time, OT will transform those operations so that they can both be applied correctly to the document, avoiding conflicts.

2. **Conflict-free Replicated Data Types (CRDTs)**:
   - o **Description**: CRDTs are a set of data structures designed to automatically resolve conflicts in distributed systems without needing a central server. They are particularly useful for real-time collaboration where you have multiple copies of data.
   - o **How it Works**: CRDTs allow different users to make updates to the same data without worrying about conflict resolution. The data structures ensure that all changes eventually converge to a consistent state.

3. **Versioning**:
   - o **Description**: This method involves creating versions of the document each time a change is

made. The system keeps track of all versions and can merge changes later.

- o **How it Works**: Each user's changes are treated as a separate version. When conflicts occur, the system can present users with options to resolve the conflicts, such as by choosing which version of a document to keep.

4. **Event Sourcing**:

- o **Description**: In event sourcing, all actions performed by users are recorded as **events**. Each event represents a change to the system's state, and these events can be broadcast to other users in real time.

- o **How it Works**: Instead of saving the current state of the document, the application stores a series of events. Each time a user makes a change, an event is triggered and sent to the server, which then broadcasts the event to all connected clients.

5. **WebSockets**:

- o **Description**: WebSockets allow for persistent, bidirectional communication between the client and server. This makes them ideal for real-time synchronization since changes can be pushed to all connected clients immediately after they are made.

o   **How it Works**: Each time a user makes a change, the change is sent over the WebSocket connection to the server. The server then broadcasts the change to all other connected clients.

Example: Building a Real-Time Document Editor

Now, let's build a simple real-time document editor using **Node.js** and **WebSockets**. The editor will allow multiple users to edit a document at the same time, and each user's changes will be immediately reflected on other clients.

Step-by-Step Guide

1. **Set Up Your Project**: Create a new directory and initialize a Node.js project.

```bash
bash
```

```bash
mkdir real-time-editor
cd real-time-editor
npm init -y
npm install express ws
```

2. **Create the Server**:

```javascript
javascript
```

```javascript
const express = require('express');
const WebSocket = require('ws');
const http = require('http');

// Initialize the app and server
const app = express();
const server = http.createServer(app);
const wss = new WebSocket.Server({ server });

let documentContent = "This is a collaborative
document.\nStart editing...";

// Serve the HTML page
app.get('/', (req, res) => {
  res.sendFile(__dirname + '/index.html');
});

// WebSocket connection handler
wss.on('connection', (ws) => {
  console.log('A new user connected');

  // Send current document content to the new
client
  ws.send(documentContent);

  // Handle incoming messages (document changes)
  ws.on('message', (message) => {
    console.log('Received message:', message);
```

```
    // Update the document content and broadcast
it to all clients
    documentContent = message;
    wss.clients.forEach(client => {
      if (client !== ws && client.readyState ===
WebSocket.OPEN) {
        client.send(message);
      }
    });
  });


  // Handle client disconnection
  ws.on('close', () => {
    console.log('A user disconnected');
  });
});

// Start the server
server.listen(8080, () => {
  console.log('Server          running          at
http://localhost:8080');
});
```

Explanation:

- The server is built using **Express** to serve the HTML file and **WebSocket (ws)** to handle real-time communication between clients.

- **documentContent** holds the content of the document, which is shared across all clients.
- When a new WebSocket connection is established, the current document content is sent to the new client.
- When a client sends an update (a new document content), it's broadcast to all other connected clients.

3. **Create the HTML Client** (index.html):

html

```
<!DOCTYPE html>
<html lang="en">
<head>
  <meta charset="UTF-8">
  <meta name="viewport" content="width=device-
width, initial-scale=1.0">
  <title>Real-Time Document Editor</title>
</head>
<body>
  <h1>Real-Time Document Editor</h1>
  <textarea id="editor" style="width: 100%;
height: 300px;"></textarea>

  <script>
    const ws = new
WebSocket('ws://localhost:8080');
    const editor =
document.getElementById('editor');
```

```javascript
    // When WebSocket connection opens, send the
current document content
    ws.onopen = () => {
      console.log('Connected to WebSocket');
    };

    // When a message is received, update the
document content
    ws.onmessage = (event) => {
      editor.value = event.data;
    };

    // Send changes to the server whenever the
user types in the editor
    editor.addEventListener('input', () => {
      const content = editor.value;
      ws.send(content);  // Send updated content
to the server
    });
  </script>
</body>
</html>
```

Explanation:

- The frontend consists of a **textarea** where users can edit the document.

- The **WebSocket connection** is established when the page loads, and the current document content is retrieved from the server.
- Every time the user types something (detected by the `input` event), the new content is sent to the server, which then broadcasts it to all connected clients.

4. Run the Server:

Run the server with the following command:

```bash
node server.js
```

Now, you can open multiple browser windows and navigate to `http://localhost:8080`. You should be able to edit the document in real time, and any changes made by one user will instantly appear for all other users.

Key Takeaways from the Example:

- **WebSocket Communication**: We use **WebSockets** to establish a persistent connection between the server and the clients. This allows us to broadcast changes in real-time to all connected clients.

- **Real-Time Document Editing**: The example allows multiple users to edit the document simultaneously, and all users stay in sync with each other.
- **Scalability**: As the application grows, you can enhance it with more advanced real-time synchronization techniques, such as **operational transformation (OT)** or **CRDTs**, to ensure conflict-free concurrent editing.

Conclusion

- **Collaborative Applications** allow multiple users to interact with the same data in real time, and they are essential in today's interactive digital ecosystem.
- **Real-Time Synchronization Techniques** such as **OT**, **CRDTs**, and **WebSockets** ensure that users can collaborate seamlessly without data conflicts or lag.
- In the **real-time document editor example**, we demonstrated how to implement basic real-time collaboration using **WebSockets** and a simple broadcast mechanism.

With the foundation laid, you can further improve the application by implementing more complex features like user presence indicators, offline support, and conflict resolution mechanisms, ensuring a robust real-time collaborative experience.

CHAPTER 16

DEPLOYING REAL-TIME APPLICATIONS

Deploying real-time applications requires careful planning to ensure they are scalable, performant, and reliable. In this chapter, we will explore how to choose a **deployment platform**, set up a **production environment**, and implement **continuous integration** for real-time apps.

Choosing a Deployment Platform

When it comes to deploying a real-time application, several cloud platforms offer tools, infrastructure, and services that can help you manage and scale your app. Below are some of the most popular platforms for deploying Node.js-based real-time applications.

1. **Heroku**:
   - o **Overview**: Heroku is a platform-as-a-service (PaaS) that provides an easy way to deploy and manage applications without having to manage infrastructure.
   - o **Why use it**: Heroku simplifies deployment with an easy-to-use interface and integrations with various add-ons (databases, caching, monitoring,

etc.). It also supports automatic scaling and provides an intuitive CI/CD pipeline.

o **Best for**: Developers who want to quickly deploy applications without managing servers.

Deploying a Node.js app on Heroku:

o Install the **Heroku CLI** and log in:

```bash

heroku login
```

o Initialize a Git repository and push your application to Heroku:

```bash

git init
heroku create your-app-name
git add .
git commit -m "Initial commit"
git push heroku master
```

o Your app will be live on Heroku after deployment. You can view logs, scale dynos (containers), and manage the app through the Heroku dashboard.

2. **Amazon Web Services (AWS)**:

o **Overview**: AWS is a comprehensive cloud platform offering various services to host and scale applications. AWS provides full control over your infrastructure with powerful compute, storage, and database options.

o **Why use it**: AWS offers powerful features for scaling, managing traffic, and maintaining high availability. It is ideal for large-scale, highly customizable applications.

o **Best for**: Developers who need full control over their infrastructure and want to scale their applications on demand.

Deploying a Node.js app on AWS EC2:

o Create an EC2 instance with an Ubuntu operating system (or any preferred OS).

o SSH into the instance:

```bash
```

```bash
ssh -i your-key.pem ubuntu@your-ec2-ip
```

o Install **Node.js** and your app's dependencies:

```bash
```

```
sudo apt update
sudo apt install nodejs npm
git clone https://github.com/your-
repository.git
cd your-repository
npm install
```

o Run your app using a process manager like **PM2** to keep the app running:

```
bash
```

```
sudo npm install -g pm2
pm2 start app.js
```

o Set up an **Elastic Load Balancer** (ELB) and **Auto Scaling** to handle increased traffic and scale horizontally across multiple instances.

3. **DigitalOcean**:

o **Overview**: DigitalOcean is a cloud infrastructure provider that makes it easy to deploy applications. It offers flexible and cost-effective options for small to medium-sized apps.

o **Why use it**: DigitalOcean offers simple virtual private servers (called Droplets) that can easily be scaled, along with managed databases and storage options.

171

o **Best for**: Developers who want simplicity and cost-effectiveness while still having control over the infrastructure.

Deploying a Node.js app on DigitalOcean:

o Create a **Droplet** instance and access it via SSH.

o Install **Node.js** and **Nginx** for reverse proxy:

bash

```
sudo apt update
sudo apt install nodejs npm nginx
```

o Deploy your app by cloning it from a Git repository, installing dependencies, and running the app:

bash

```
git clone https://github.com/your-
repository.git
cd your-repository
npm install
node app.js
```

o Use **Nginx** to route HTTP traffic to your Node.js app and set up SSL certificates if needed.

4. **Google Cloud Platform (GCP)**:

o **Overview**: GCP provides a suite of tools for cloud computing, storage, and machine learning. It offers services like **Google Kubernetes Engine (GKE)** for containerized applications and **App Engine** for simple web app hosting.

o **Why use it**: GCP's Kubernetes tools and AI capabilities are ideal for highly scalable and complex real-time applications.

o **Best for**: Developers building large, complex applications with high scalability needs.

Deploying a Node.js app on GCP:

o Use **Google Cloud Storage** for file storage and **Cloud Pub/Sub** for message queues.

o Deploy your app using **Google App Engine**:

```bash
```

```
gcloud app create
gcloud app deploy
```

Setting Up a Production Environment

Setting up a production environment is crucial to ensure that your real-time application runs smoothly and securely. Here's how to set up the production environment for a Node.js app:

173

1. **Environment Variables**: Use environment variables to store sensitive data (such as API keys, database credentials, and JWT secrets). This helps keep the configuration secure and adaptable across different environments (development, staging, production).

   o Create a .env file and use the **dotenv** package to load environment variables:

   bash

   ```
   npm install dotenv
   ```

   In your Node.js app:

   javascript

   ```
   require('dotenv').config();

   const            dbPassword            =
   process.env.DB_PASSWORD;
   ```

2. **Use a Process Manager (PM2)**: In production, you want your Node.js app to be always running, and **PM2** is an excellent tool for that. PM2 can automatically restart your app if it crashes and manage logs.

   o Install PM2 globally:

   bash

```
npm install -g pm2
```

o   Start your app with PM2:

```
bash
```

```
pm2 start app.js --name "real-time-
app"
pm2 save  # Saves the process list to
restart on reboot
pm2 startup  # Configure PM2 to start
on system boot
```

3. **Reverse Proxy with Nginx**: Nginx can be used to serve your Node.js app by acting as a reverse proxy. This helps distribute traffic efficiently and adds a layer of security and flexibility.

   Example Nginx configuration (/etc/nginx/sites-available/default):

```
nginx
```

```
server {
  listen 80;
  server_name your-domain.com;

  location / {
```

175

```
    proxy_pass http://127.0.0.1:3000;    #
Node.js app is running on port 3000
    proxy_http_version 1.1;
    proxy_set_header               Upgrade
$http_upgrade;
    proxy_set_header Connection 'upgrade';
    proxy_set_header Host $host;
    proxy_cache_bypass $http_upgrade;
  }
}
```

4. **Database Configuration**:
   - Use **MongoDB Atlas**, **RDS**, or other cloud database services for scalable and managed databases in production.
   - Ensure that your database is properly indexed for performance and backup systems are in place.

5. **Security**:
   - Enable **SSL/TLS encryption** to secure communication between clients and your server. You can use **Let's Encrypt** for free SSL certificates.
   - Implement **firewall rules** and ensure that only necessary ports (such as 80 for HTTP and 443 for HTTPS) are open.
   - Use **CORS (Cross-Origin Resource Sharing)** headers to restrict which domains can access your APIs.

o Set up **Rate Limiting** to prevent abuse of your APIs.

Continuous Integration for Real-Time Apps

Continuous Integration (CI) helps automate the testing, building, and deployment process for your Node.js real-time application. This is especially important for real-time applications, where updates need to be deployed frequently without downtime.

1. **Set Up a CI Pipeline**: Use a CI tool such as **GitHub Actions**, **Travis CI**, or **CircleCI** to automate your deployment process.

   Example using GitHub Actions:

   o Create a `.github/workflows/node.js.yml` file to define your CI pipeline:

   ```yaml
   yaml


   name: Node.js CI


   on:
     push:
       branches:
         - main
   ```

```
jobs:
  build:
    runs-on: ubuntu-latest

    steps:
    - name: Checkout code
      uses: actions/checkout@v2

    - name: Set up Node.js
      uses: actions/setup-node@v2
      with:
        node-version: '14'

    - name: Install dependencies
      run: npm install

    - name: Run tests
      run: npm test

    - name: Deploy to Heroku
      uses:      akshnz/heroku-deploy-action@v1.0.3
      with:
        heroku_api_key:            ${{
secrets.HEROKU_API_KEY }}
        heroku_app_name:        your-heroku-app-name
```

Explanation:

o **GitHub Actions** runs your CI pipeline when code is pushed to the `main` branch.

o The pipeline checks out the code, installs dependencies, runs tests, and then deploys to **Heroku**.

o Secrets (like **HEROKU_API_KEY**) should be stored securely in GitHub's secret settings.

2. **Automated Testing**: Use testing libraries like **Mocha**, **Chai**, or **Jest** to create unit and integration tests for your Node.js app. Run tests in the CI pipeline to ensure that new changes don't break functionality.

Example test with **Jest**:

javascript

```
test('adds 1 + 2 to equal 3', () => {
  expect(1 + 2).toBe(3);
});
```

3. **Deploy to Production**: The CI pipeline can automatically deploy your app to the production environment (Heroku, AWS, etc.) once tests pass. This ensures that your application is always up-to-date without manual intervention.

Summary

- **Choosing a Deployment Platform**: Depending on your needs, platforms like **Heroku** (easy setup), **AWS** (powerful, customizable), and **DigitalOcean** (simple) are popular choices for deploying Node.js applications.

- **Setting Up a Production Environment**: Ensure your production environment is secure, efficient, and scalable by using tools like **PM2, Nginx, SSL/TLS encryption**, and **cloud databases**.

- **Continuous Integration**: Automate your deployment process with **CI tools** like GitHub Actions, ensuring that changes are tested and deployed seamlessly, minimizing downtime and bugs.

By implementing the right deployment and CI strategies, you can ensure that your real-time application is always up, performing well, and secure for users.

CHAPTER 17

MONITORING AND LOGGING IN REAL-TIME SYSTEMS

In real-time applications, it's critical to have robust **monitoring** and **logging** in place to ensure that your system is functioning as expected. Logs help you track what happens in the application, detect issues early, and debug problems that occur in production. In this chapter, we'll cover how to implement logging with **Winston** and **Morgan**, explore **real-time monitoring tools**, and discuss best practices for **debugging and handling errors in production**.

Implementing Logging with Winston and Morgan

Logging plays an essential role in tracking system events, errors, and user activity in real-time systems. Two of the most commonly used logging libraries for Node.js are **Winston** and **Morgan**.

1. **Winston**:
   - o **Overview**: Winston is a versatile logging library that supports multiple transports (e.g., logging to the console, files, or external services like AWS CloudWatch, Loggly, etc.).

o **Why use it**: Winston is highly configurable, supports log levels, and allows you to format and transport logs to multiple destinations.

Setting up Winston: Install Winston:

```bash
npm install winston
```

Example usage in your Node.js app:

```javascript
const winston = require('winston');

// Create a Winston logger
const logger = winston.createLogger({
  level: 'info',  // The lowest level to
log (info, warn, error)
  transports: [
    // Log to the console
    new winston.transports.Console({
      format: winston.format.combine(
        winston.format.colorize(),      //
Adds color to log levels
        winston.format.simple()         //
Simple format
      ),
    }),
```

```
// Log to a file
new              winston.transports.File({
filename: 'app.log' }),
  ],
});


// Example logging
logger.info('This    is    an    informational
message.');
logger.warn('This is a warning message.');
logger.error('This is an error message.');
```

Explanation:

- o **level**: Defines the minimum level of logs to capture. The levels in order of severity are `error, warn, info, http, verbose, debug,` and `silly`.

- o **transports**: Defines where the logs are stored or displayed. In this case, logs are shown on the console and written to a file.

- o **Log Levels**: You can choose to log different types of events, such as informational messages, warnings, and errors.

2. **Morgan**:

- o **Overview**: Morgan is an HTTP request logger middleware for Node.js. It is often used in Express apps to log incoming HTTP requests.

183

- o **Why use it**: It provides detailed logs about each HTTP request, including status codes, request times, and response sizes.

Setting up Morgan: Install Morgan:

bash

```
npm install morgan
```

Example usage in your Express app:

javascript

```
const express = require('express');
const morgan = require('morgan');
const app = express();

// Setup Morgan to log requests to the
console
app.use(morgan('combined'));        //
'combined' provides detailed logs

// Example route
app.get('/', (req, res) => {
  res.send('Hello, world!');
});

// Start the server
app.listen(3000, () => {
```

```
console.log('Server    running    on    port
3000');
});
```

Explanation:

- ○ **morgan('combined')**: This preset logs information like HTTP method, URL, status code, and response time in a standard format. Other formats like dev and tiny are also available.

- ○ **Request Logging**: This middleware automatically logs every incoming HTTP request, providing valuable insight into client-server interactions.

Real-Time Monitoring Tools and Techniques

Monitoring is essential to ensure your real-time application is running smoothly and that any issues are detected early. Below are some tools and techniques for monitoring Node.js real-time applications:

1. **New Relic**:

- ○ **Overview**: New Relic is a powerful application performance monitoring (APM) tool that offers real-time analytics and detailed monitoring of your application's performance.

185

o **Why use it**: New Relic provides in-depth performance metrics like response time, throughput, error rates, and transaction tracing, which are invaluable for real-time apps.

Integrating New Relic:

o Install the New Relic Node.js agent:

```bash
npm install newrelic
```

o Create a `newrelic.js` configuration file and add your New Relic license key.
o Add the following code at the very top of your main application file (e.g., `app.js` or `server.js`):

```javascript
require('newrelic');
```

New Relic will now start monitoring your application and provide detailed performance data.

2. **Prometheus and Grafana**:
   o **Overview**: Prometheus is an open-source monitoring system and time-series database that

is ideal for gathering metrics from real-time applications. Grafana is often used in conjunction with Prometheus to visualize the data.

o **Why use it**: Prometheus collects metrics such as CPU usage, memory, and custom application metrics, while Grafana allows you to create real-time dashboards to visualize these metrics.

Integrating Prometheus with Node.js:

o Install the Prometheus client for Node.js:

```bash
```

```bash
npm install prom-client
```

o Create a simple endpoint that exposes application metrics:

```javascript
```

```javascript
const express = require('express');
const { collectDefaultMetrics,
Registry, Gauge } = require('prom-
client');

const app = express();
const registry = new Registry();
```

```
// Collect default metrics (CPU,
memory, etc.)
collectDefaultMetrics({   register:
registry });

// Custom metric: number of active
users
const activeUsers = new Gauge({
  name: 'active_users',
  help: 'Number of active users',
});
activeUsers.set(10);   // Example
value

// Expose metrics at /metrics
endpoint
app.get('/metrics', async (req, res)
=> {
  res.set('Content-Type',
registry.contentType);
  res.end(await registry.metrics());
});

app.listen(3000, () => {
  console.log('Server running on
port 3000');
});
```

Explanation:

- o **Prometheus** collects metrics like CPU and memory usage with `collectDefaultMetrics()`.
- o **Custom Metrics** can be added, like the number of active users (shown here with the `activeUsers` Gauge).
- o The `/metrics` endpoint exposes all the collected data, which can be scraped by Prometheus for real-time monitoring.

After scraping the data, you can visualize the metrics in **Grafana**, creating real-time dashboards for monitoring your Node.js app.

3. **Datadog**:
- o **Overview**: Datadog is a popular cloud-based monitoring and analytics platform that provides real-time visibility into the performance of your applications, servers, and databases.
- o **Why use it**: Datadog integrates well with Node.js and provides tools for tracking errors, latency, throughput, and other critical metrics.
- o **Integrating Datadog**: You can use the **Datadog Node.js agent** to monitor your application, and Datadog offers integrations with various other services and databases to provide a comprehensive monitoring solution.

Debugging and Handling Errors in Production

When running a real-time application in production, issues are bound to arise. Efficient debugging and error handling are key to keeping your app running smoothly. Below are some best practices for debugging and handling errors in production:

1. **Centralized Error Logging**: In production, it's critical to have centralized error logging to quickly detect and address issues. Use services like **Loggly**, **Papertrail**, or **Elasticsearch** combined with **Winston** to capture logs and monitor them in real time.

   Example of centralized logging setup in Winston:

   ```javascript
   const winston = require('winston');
   require('winston-daily-rotate-file');   //
   Rotate logs daily

   const logger = winston.createLogger({
     level: 'info',
     format: winston.format.json(),
     transports: [
       new winston.transports.Console(),
       new
   winston.transports.DailyRotateFile({
         filename: 'logs/app-%DATE%.log',
   ```

```
     datePattern: 'YYYY-MM-DD',
     zippedArchive: true,
     maxSize: '20m',
     maxFiles: '14d',
   }),
 ],
});


logger.error('This is an error message');
```

Explanation:

- o **Daily Rotate File**: Winston's `DailyRotateFile` transport creates log files that rotate daily, keeping them organized.
- o Centralized logging helps in identifying trends in errors and provides context for debugging in production.

2. **Error Handling Middleware (Express)**: In an Express app, you should have a centralized error handling middleware to catch unhandled errors and send proper responses to the client.

```javascript
app.use((err, req, res, next) => {
  console.error(err.stack);   // Log the
error stack
```

```
res.status(500).send('Something      went
wrong!');  // Send a generic error response
});
```

Explanation:

- o This middleware catches any errors that are passed along using next(err) and logs them.
- o It also ensures that the user is notified with a general error message, while the detailed error is logged for internal tracking.

3. **Handling Uncaught Exceptions and Rejections**: Make sure to handle uncaught exceptions and unhandled promise rejections. In production, it's essential to catch these errors to prevent your app from crashing.

```javascript
process.on('uncaughtException', (err) => {
  console.error('Uncaught      exception:',
err);
  // Optionally, send an alert to an admin
  process.exit(1);  // Exit the process
after logging the error
});

process.on('unhandledRejection', (reason,
promise) => {
```

```
console.error('Unhandled          promise
rejection:', reason);
// Optionally, send an alert to an admin
process.exit(1);    // Exit the process
after logging the error
});
```

Explanation:

- o By listening for uncaughtException and unhandledRejection, you can log critical errors and safely shut down the process or restart it using process managers like **PM2**.

Summary

- **Logging** with **Winston** and **Morgan** provides essential insights into the application's behavior and helps with debugging in real-time systems.
- **Real-time monitoring** tools like **New Relic**, **Prometheus**, and **Datadog** help track performance metrics, errors, and usage patterns, allowing you to respond quickly to issues.
- **Debugging and error handling** in production are critical for maintaining a smooth user experience. Use centralized logging, proper error handling middleware, and safeguard against uncaught exceptions and unhandled promise rejections to ensure stability in your real-time application.

With effective monitoring, logging, and error management in place, you can proactively address issues, ensuring that your real-time application is resilient and scalable.

CHAPTER 18

OPTIMIZING PERFORMANCE IN REAL-TIME NODE.JS APPS

In real-time applications, performance is crucial. Since these applications often require low-latency responses and high throughput (e.g., real-time messaging, live updates, and collaboration), identifying and optimizing performance bottlenecks in **Node.js** is essential. In this chapter, we will cover:

1. **Performance bottlenecks in Node.js**.
2. **Optimizing the event loop and I/O operations**.
3. **Tools for performance profiling**.

Performance Bottlenecks in Node.js

Node.js is designed to handle high concurrency efficiently, thanks to its **event-driven, non-blocking I/O model**. However, despite its efficiency, certain aspects of your app can still become performance bottlenecks. Below are common bottlenecks in Node.js applications:

1. **Blocking the Event Loop**:
   o The event loop is responsible for handling I/O operations, network requests, and events

asynchronously. If a long-running, CPU-bound task (like complex calculations or synchronous blocking operations) is executed on the main thread, it can **block the event loop**, causing delays for all other operations.

- o **Example**: A synchronous `for` loop with heavy computation can block the event loop, delaying the processing of incoming requests.

2. **Database Latency**:

- o **Database queries**, especially those that involve large datasets or slow network connections, can introduce significant latency in real-time applications.
- o If your application makes synchronous database queries or doesn't handle database connections efficiently, the user experience will suffer.

3. **Memory Leaks**:

- o Memory leaks can occur when your app holds onto memory unnecessarily, causing the memory footprint to grow over time. This leads to slower performance and potential application crashes.
- o Memory leaks are more prevalent in long-running processes like real-time servers where many connections are open at once.

4. **Inefficient Networking**:

- o In real-time applications, networking (e.g., WebSocket connections) is critical. If the network layer isn't optimized (e.g., by maintaining too many open connections or sending too much data unnecessarily), it can lead to slowdowns.

5. **Large Payloads**:
   - o Transmitting large data payloads in real-time (e.g., large messages, file uploads) can overload the system and network bandwidth, affecting performance.

Optimizing Event Loop and I/O Operations

Optimizing the **event loop** and **I/O operations** is key to improving Node.js performance. Since Node.js is single-threaded, all operations must be efficiently managed to avoid blocking the event loop.

1. **Non-Blocking I/O Operations**:
   - o **Always use asynchronous operations** (like `fs.readFile` instead of `fs.readFileSync`) for file I/O, network requests, and database operations. This ensures that the event loop is free to handle other tasks while waiting for these operations to complete.

197

Example: Using async file reading:

```javascript
const fs = require('fs');

// Non-blocking I/O
fs.readFile('file.txt', 'utf8', (err,
data) => {
  if (err) {
    console.error('Error reading file:',
err);
  } else {
    console.log('File content:', data);
  }
});
```

2. **Offloading CPU-bound Tasks**:
   o   For CPU-heavy tasks (such as image processing or large calculations), offload these tasks to a separate thread or use **Node.js worker threads** or **child processes**. This prevents blocking the event loop and allows the main thread to remain responsive.

Example: Using Worker Threads:

```javascript
```

```javascript
const { Worker, isMainThread, parentPort }
= require('worker_threads');

if (isMainThread) {
  // Create a worker thread
  const worker = new Worker(__filename);
  worker.on('message', (result) => {
    console.log('Result   from   worker:',
result);
  });
  worker.postMessage('start');
} else {
  // Worker thread logic
  parentPort.on('message', (message) => {
    if (message === 'start') {
      const            result           =
performHeavyComputation();
      parentPort.postMessage(result);
    }
  });

  function performHeavyComputation() {
    let sum = 0;
    for (let i = 0; i < 1e6; i++) {
      sum += i;
    }
    return sum;
  }
}
```

199

Explanation:

- o **Worker Threads** allow CPU-intensive tasks to run in parallel, keeping the event loop free. Workers communicate with the main thread via message passing.

3. **Use Efficient Data Structures**:
   - o **Avoid using inefficient algorithms** or data structures that require excessive time or memory. Opt for more efficient algorithms when working with large datasets (e.g., using hashmaps for lookups instead of arrays).

4. **Use Caching**:
   - o Implement caching for data that doesn't change often (e.g., static content or frequent database queries). Tools like **Redis** or **Memcached** can drastically reduce the load on your database by serving cached responses for repeated queries.

Example: Caching with Redis:

javascript

```
const redis = require('redis');
const client = redis.createClient();

// Check if data is cached
client.get('someKey', (err, reply) => {
```

```
if (reply) {
  console.log('Cache hit:', reply);
} else {
  console.log('Cache    miss,    querying
database...');
  // Query your database here and cache
the result
  const dbResult = 'someData';
  client.setex('someKey',           3600,
dbResult);  // Cache for 1 hour
  }
});
```

5. **Optimize Network Calls**:

   o **Reduce unnecessary network calls** and batch requests when possible to minimize latency. You can also use techniques like **long polling, WebSockets,** or **Server-Sent Events (SSE)** to push updates to clients in real time rather than frequently querying the server.

Tools for Performance Profiling

To identify performance bottlenecks and optimize your real-time application, you can use various profiling tools. These tools help you understand how your application is using resources and where it can be improved.

1. **Node.js Built-in Profiler**:

o Node.js provides built-in profiling capabilities via the `--inspect` flag, which allows you to inspect performance and debug the app.

Example:

```bash
```

```bash
node --inspect app.js
```

o This starts the app in inspection mode, and you can connect it to Chrome DevTools or use the `node --inspect-brk` option to pause execution at the start.

2. **The `clinic.js` Tool**:

o **Clinic.js** is a powerful tool for profiling and diagnosing performance issues in Node.js applications. It provides visualizations of your application's event loop, CPU usage, memory consumption, and more.

Example:

```bash
```

```bash
npm install -g clinic
clinic doctor -- node app.js
```

o After running the tool, it will generate a report that helps you identify performance bottlenecks.

3. **New Relic or Datadog**:

o These application performance monitoring (APM) tools provide real-time insights into your application's performance. They can monitor memory usage, response times, error rates, and more.

o **New Relic** provides in-depth profiling, transaction tracing, and detailed performance metrics.

o **Datadog** offers monitoring and analytics, allowing you to track key metrics, including response times, latency, and throughput, across distributed systems.

4. **Chrome DevTools**:

o Chrome DevTools can be used for profiling Node.js applications by connecting to the app via the `--inspect` flag. This allows you to inspect the call stack, event loop, and memory usage in real-time.

Steps:

o Start your app with the `--inspect` flag:

```bash
bash
```

```
node --inspect app.js
```

- o Open `chrome://inspect` in Chrome and click on "Inspect" to view the Node.js application's execution details.

5. **PM2 with Keymetrics**:
   - o **PM2** is a process manager for Node.js applications that also provides monitoring capabilities. You can use it in combination with **Keymetrics**, a service that offers real-time performance monitoring, memory, and CPU usage tracking.

Example:

```
bash

pm2 start app.js
pm2 monit  # To view live metrics
```

6. **Heapdump**:
   - o **Heapdump** is a module for Node.js that helps you take heap snapshots of your application. This can help you analyze memory leaks by comparing memory usage over time.

Example:

```bash
bash

npm install heapdump
const heapdump = require('heapdump');

// Take a snapshot of the current heap
memory
heapdump.writeSnapshot('/path/to/snapshot
.heapsnapshot');
```

You can then analyze these heap snapshots using Chrome DevTools.

Summary

- **Performance Bottlenecks** in Node.js are often caused by blocking the event loop with synchronous operations, inefficient I/O handling, and excessive memory usage. Avoid blocking operations and use asynchronous I/O operations to keep the event loop responsive.
- **Optimizing Event Loop and I/O Operations** involves offloading CPU-bound tasks to worker threads, using non-blocking I/O, caching, and optimizing network calls.
- **Tools for Performance Profiling** such as the built-in **Node.js profiler**, **Clinic.js**, **New Relic**, and **Datadog** can help identify performance bottlenecks and improve the efficiency of your Node.js real-time applications.

By implementing these optimizations, you can ensure that your real-time Node.js applications perform efficiently, scale well under heavy load, and provide a responsive user experience.

CHAPTER 19

HANDLING HIGH TRAFFIC WITH NODE.JS

Handling high traffic in real-time applications is a crucial task, especially when dealing with large-scale systems or when your app is expected to handle thousands or even millions of concurrent users. **Node.js**, with its event-driven, non-blocking architecture, is well-suited for handling high concurrency, but additional strategies are necessary to ensure optimal performance under heavy traffic. In this chapter, we'll explore **strategies for handling large-scale traffic**, **caching strategies to improve performance**, and **rate limiting** to protect your APIs.

Strategies for Handling Large-Scale Traffic

When dealing with high traffic, your application needs to be designed to efficiently manage large numbers of requests and concurrent connections. Below are several strategies to help you handle large-scale traffic in a Node.js application:

1. **Horizontal Scaling**:
    o **Why it works**: Node.js is single-threaded, so using multiple server instances across multiple machines (or containers) can increase your app's

capacity to handle more traffic. **Horizontal scaling** allows you to distribute the load across multiple processes or machines.

- o **How to implement**:
  - Use the **Node.js cluster module** to spawn multiple worker processes on each server, and distribute requests across them.
  - Use a **load balancer** (e.g., **NGINX**, **HAProxy**) to distribute traffic across multiple server instances.

Example using NGINX as a load balancer:

```nginx
upstream node_app {
  server 127.0.0.1:3000;
  server 127.0.0.1:3001;
  server 127.0.0.1:3002;
}

server {
  listen 80;

  location / {
    proxy_pass http://node_app;
    proxy_set_header Host $host;
```

```
    proxy_set_header           X-Real-IP
$remote_addr;
    proxy_set_header       X-Forwarded-For
$proxy_add_x_forwarded_for;
    proxy_set_header     X-Forwarded-Proto
$scheme;
  }
}
```

This configuration allows NGINX to distribute traffic to three different Node.js instances running on different ports.

2. **Load Balancing**:

   o **Why it works**: Load balancing ensures that no single server or process is overwhelmed by traffic. It distributes incoming requests evenly among available servers or containers.

   o **How to implement**: You can configure a load balancer to distribute traffic using various strategies:

     ▪ **Round-robin**: Requests are distributed evenly across all available servers.

     ▪ **Least Connections**: Traffic is directed to the server with the fewest active connections.

209

- **IP Hashing**: Requests from the same client IP are routed to the same server, which is useful for session persistence.

3. **Service-Oriented Architecture (SOA)**:
   - **Why it works**: Instead of one monolithic application, break your system into smaller, manageable microservices that can be scaled independently. Each microservice handles a specific function of your application (e.g., authentication, payment processing, user management).
   - **How to implement**: Use **Docker** containers to deploy each microservice, and **Kubernetes** to manage and scale these services across multiple machines.

4. **Serverless Architecture**:
   - **Why it works**: With **serverless** computing, you can offload scaling and management to cloud providers like **AWS Lambda**, **Azure Functions**, or **Google Cloud Functions**. This is ideal for handling variable or unpredictable traffic.
   - **How to implement**: Deploy your app's critical functions (e.g., image processing, data aggregation) in serverless environments where the cloud provider automatically scales the resources based on traffic.

5. **Connection Pooling**:

   o **Why it works**: Maintaining multiple concurrent connections to services like databases or APIs can create a bottleneck. Using **connection pooling** reduces the overhead of establishing new connections for each request.

   o **How to implement**: Most database clients (e.g., **MongoDB, PostgreSQL**) provide connection pooling mechanisms that allow you to reuse connections instead of opening a new one for each request.

Caching Strategies to Improve Performance

Caching is a powerful technique for improving the performance of your application, especially under high traffic. By storing the results of frequently requested data, you reduce the need for repetitive computations or database queries.

1. **In-Memory Caching**:

   o **Why it works**: Storing frequently accessed data in memory (such as **Redis** or **Memcached**) significantly reduces access time, as retrieving data from memory is much faster than querying a database.

   o **How to implement**:

- Use **Redis** to store key-value pairs. For example, cache frequently accessed data like user profiles, session information, or search results.

Example with Redis:

javascript

```javascript
const redis = require('redis');
const client = redis.createClient();

// Set a cache key with an expiration time
(e.g., 1 hour)
client.setex('user:123',             3600,
JSON.stringify({ name: 'John Doe', age: 30
}));

// Retrieve the cached data
client.get('user:123', (err, reply) => {
  if (reply) {
    console.log('Cache              hit:',
JSON.parse(reply));
  } else {
    console.log('Cache miss');
    // Query the database and cache the
result
  }
});
```

2. **HTTP Caching**:

   o **Why it works**: HTTP caching is an essential strategy for reducing the load on your web server by caching the responses to HTTP requests.

   o **How to implement**:

      ▪ Use HTTP headers like `Cache-Control`, `ETag`, or `Last-Modified` to specify how and for how long responses should be cached.

      ▪ Leverage **CDNs** (Content Delivery Networks) for caching static resources (e.g., images, CSS files, JavaScript) at edge locations to reduce the load on the server.

   Example HTTP Cache-Control Header:

   javascript

```javascript
app.get('/static-file', (req, res) => {
  res.setHeader('Cache-Control', 'public,
max-age=86400'); // Cache for 1 day
  res.sendFile('/path/to/file');
});
```

3. **Database Caching**:

213

- o **Why it works**: By caching the results of database queries, you reduce the load on the database and improve response times.
- o **How to implement**:
  - Use **Redis** to cache the results of database queries, especially for frequently accessed data that doesn't change often.
  - For **MongoDB**, use **MongoDB Atlas** with **Global Clusters** to cache data across multiple regions, minimizing latency.

Rate Limiting and Protecting APIs

When your application faces high traffic, you need to implement **rate limiting** to prevent abuse, ensure fair resource usage, and protect your APIs from overuse or **Denial of Service (DoS)** attacks.

1. **Rate Limiting**:
   - o **Why it works**: Rate limiting ensures that clients can only make a certain number of requests within a defined time period (e.g., 100 requests per minute). This helps prevent **DoS attacks** and ensures fair usage of server resources.
   - o **How to implement**:

- Use libraries like **express-rate-limit** to limit the number of requests a user can make to your API.

Example with express-rate-limit:

bash

```
npm install express-rate-limit
javascript
```

```javascript
const rateLimit = require('express-rate-limit');
const express = require('express');
const app = express();

// Apply rate limit to all API requests
const limiter = rateLimit({
  windowMs: 15 * 60 * 1000,  // 15 minutes
  max: 100,   // Limit each IP to 100 requests per windowMs
  message: 'Too many requests, please try again later.',
});

app.use('/api/', limiter);

app.get('/api/data', (req, res) => {
  res.json({ data: 'This is some data' });
```

```
});

app.listen(3000, () => {
  console.log('Server   running   on   port
3000');
});
```

Explanation:

- This code limits the number of requests an IP can make to 100 per 15 minutes.
- If the limit is exceeded, the server responds with a message indicating too many requests.

2. **Protecting APIs with Authentication**:
   - **Why it works**: API security is critical for preventing unauthorized access. By enforcing authentication (e.g., using JWTs) and requiring API keys, you can ensure that only authorized users can access sensitive endpoints.
   - **How to implement**:
     - Use **JWT (JSON Web Tokens)** to authenticate API requests and authorize access to specific routes.
     - Use **API keys** for external services to monitor and limit usage.

Example with JWT Authentication:

```javascript
javascript

const jwt = require('jsonwebtoken');
const express = require('express');
const app = express();

// Middleware to authenticate API requests
const authenticateJWT = (req, res, next) =>
{
  const                token                =
req.header('Authorization').split(' ')[1];
  if (!token) return res.sendStatus(403);

  jwt.verify(token,      'your-secret-key',
(err, user) => {
    if (err) return res.sendStatus(403);
    req.user = user;
    next();
  });
};

app.get('/protected',      authenticateJWT,
(req, res) => {
  res.send('This is a protected route');
});

app.listen(3000, () => {
  console.log('Server   running   on   port
3000');
```

```
});
```

Summary

- **Strategies for Handling Large-Scale Traffic** include horizontal scaling (using multiple instances), load balancing (using NGINX or similar), and containerized services (using Kubernetes or Docker).

- **Caching Strategies** (e.g., Redis, HTTP caching, database caching) reduce the load on your server and improve response times, especially for frequently accessed data.

- **Rate Limiting** ensures fair resource usage and protects your APIs from abuse. Tools like **express-rate-limit** help you limit the number of requests from each user.

By implementing these techniques, you can build scalable and high-performing Node.js applications that can handle high traffic and provide a seamless user experience.

CHAPTER 20

REAL-TIME VIDEO AND AUDIO STREAMING WITH NODE.JS

Real-time media streaming, such as video and audio streaming, is an essential feature for applications like video calls, live broadcasts, and collaborative meetings. In this chapter, we'll cover how to set up **real-time media streaming** with **Node.js**, use **WebRTC** (Web Real-Time Communication) for peer-to-peer communication, and build a **video call application** as a practical example.

Setting Up Real-Time Media Streaming

Real-time media streaming typically involves transmitting video and audio data between a server and clients, or directly between clients (peer-to-peer). Setting up real-time media streaming requires managing media capture, transmission, and rendering. With **Node.js**, we can leverage various tools and protocols to achieve real-time media streaming.

1. **WebRTC (Web Real-Time Communication)** is the most common technology used for real-time peer-to-peer communication. WebRTC enables direct browser-to-browser data sharing, without needing plugins or

additional software. It's widely used in applications such as video conferencing, file sharing, and live streaming.

2. **Server-Side Components**: While WebRTC handles peer-to-peer communication directly between browsers, you still need a **signaling server** to exchange metadata (such as ICE candidates and session descriptions) between peers to establish the connection.

3. **STUN/TURN Servers**: WebRTC uses **STUN (Session Traversal Utilities for NAT)** and **TURN (Traversal Using Relays around NAT)** servers to establish connectivity between peers. A STUN server helps peers discover their public IP addresses, and a TURN server is used to relay media when direct peer-to-peer communication isn't possible due to network restrictions.

Using WebRTC with Node.js

WebRTC is primarily a client-side API, but Node.js can be used to implement the signaling server and handle the exchange of metadata between clients. Here's how to set up a basic WebRTC application in Node.js:

1. **Install Dependencies**:
   o   We'll need **Express** for the signaling server and **Socket.io** for real-time communication between clients and the server.

```
bash
```

```
npm install express socket.io
```

2. **Setting Up the Signaling Server**:
   - o The signaling server will use **Socket.io** to facilitate the exchange of WebRTC signaling messages (such as ICE candidates and offer/answer SDP).

   Server-Side (Node.js with Express and Socket.io):

```javascript
const express = require('express');
const http = require('http');
const socketIo = require('socket.io');

const app = express();
const server = http.createServer(app);
const io = socketIo(server);

// Serve the client-side files (HTML, JS, etc.)
app.use(express.static('public'));

// Handle signaling messages from clients
io.on('connection', (socket) => {
  console.log('A user connected');
```

```
  // Relay messages between clients (offer,
answer, and ICE candidates)
  socket.on('offer', (offer) => {
    socket.broadcast.emit('offer', offer);
  });

  socket.on('answer', (answer) => {
    socket.broadcast.emit('answer',
answer);
  });

  socket.on('candidate', (candidate) => {
    socket.broadcast.emit('candidate',
candidate);
  });

  socket.on('disconnect', () => {
    console.log('A user disconnected');
  });
});

// Start the server
server.listen(3000, () => {
  console.log('Server       running       on
http://localhost:3000');
});
```

Explanation:

o **Socket.io** is used to handle real-time communication. When a user sends an offer, answer, or ICE candidate, the signaling server broadcasts the message to the other users.

o The server serves static files (HTML, JavaScript) to the clients, enabling the WebRTC client-side logic.

3. **Client-Side WebRTC Setup**:

o On the client side, we will use the **WebRTC API** to capture the user's webcam and microphone, establish a peer-to-peer connection, and exchange media between clients.

Client-Side (HTML and JavaScript):

html

```
<!DOCTYPE html>
<html lang="en">
<head>
  <meta charset="UTF-8">
  <meta                 name="viewport"
content="width=device-width,     initial-
scale=1.0">
  <title>Video Call</title>
</head>
<body>
  <h1>Video Call</h1>
```

```
<video      id="localVideo"      autoplay
muted></video>
<video              id="remoteVideo"
autoplay></video>
<script
src="/socket.io/socket.io.js"></script>
<script>
  const socket = io();

  const      localVideo      =
document.getElementById('localVideo');
  const      remoteVideo      =
document.getElementById('remoteVideo');

  const peerConnectionConfig = {
    iceServers: [
      {                    urls:
'stun:stun.l.google.com:19302' },
      {    urls:    'turn:your-turn-
server.com',    username:    'username',
credential: 'password' }
    ]
  };

  let localStream;
  let peerConnection;

  // Capture local video and audio
```

224

```javascript
navigator.mediaDevices.getUserMedia({
video: true, audio: true })
    .then((stream) => {
      localVideo.srcObject = stream;
      localStream = stream;
    })
    .catch((err) => {
      console.error('Error    accessing
media devices: ', err);
    });

// Create an offer and send it to the
server
    function createOffer() {
      peerConnection          =          new
RTCPeerConnection(peerConnectionConfig);

localStream.getTracks().forEach(track   =>
peerConnection.addTrack(track,
localStream));

      peerConnection.createOffer()
        .then((offer) => {
          return
peerConnection.setLocalDescription(offer)
;
        })
        .then(() => {
```

```
      socket.emit('offer',
peerConnection.localDescription);
      });

   peerConnection.onicecandidate      =
(event) => {
      if (event.candidate) {
        socket.emit('candidate',
event.candidate);
      }
   };

   peerConnection.ontrack = (event) =>
{
      remoteVideo.srcObject            =
event.streams[0];
   };
  }

  // Handle an incoming offer from
another peer
  socket.on('offer', (offer) => {
    peerConnection            =            new
RTCPeerConnection(peerConnectionConfig);

localStream.getTracks().forEach(track    =>
peerConnection.addTrack(track,
localStream));
```

226

```
peerConnection.setRemoteDescription(new
RTCSessionDescription(offer))
        .then(() => {
        return
peerConnection.createAnswer();
        })
        .then((answer) => {
        return
peerConnection.setLocalDescription(answer
);
        })
        .then(() => {
        socket.emit('answer',
peerConnection.localDescription);
        });

    peerConnection.onicecandidate      =
(event) => {
        if (event.candidate) {
        socket.emit('candidate',
event.candidate);
        }
    };

    peerConnection.ontrack = (event) =>
{
        remoteVideo.srcObject              =
event.streams[0];
```

```
        };
    });

    // Handle an incoming answer from
another peer
    socket.on('answer', (answer) => {

peerConnection.setRemoteDescription(new
RTCSessionDescription(answer));
    });

    // Handle incoming ICE candidates
    socket.on('candidate', (candidate) =>
{
        peerConnection.addIceCandidate(new
RTCIceCandidate(candidate));
    });

    // Start the call
    createOffer();
  </script>
</body>
</html>
```

Explanation:

o   The client uses **getUserMedia()** to access the
    webcam and microphone, and the video is
    displayed in the localVideo element.

- o When a user wants to make a call, they create an **offer** using **WebRTC's RTCPeerConnection**. The offer is sent to the signaling server using **Socket.io**.

- o The peer-to-peer connection is established using **WebRTC**, and the remote video stream is displayed in the `remoteVideo` element.

Example: Building a Video Call Application

In the example above, we implemented a basic **video call application** that uses **WebRTC** for real-time communication. Here's how the application works:

1. **Signaling**: The server handles the exchange of **offer, answer**, and **ICE candidates** between peers. These are necessary to establish a peer-to-peer connection.

2. **WebRTC API**: WebRTC is used on the client-side to capture the user's media (video/audio), create a peer connection, and exchange media streams between clients.

3. **Media Transmission**: Once the connection is established, the media streams (video and audio) are sent directly between clients using **peer-to-peer** communication.

Conclusion

- **WebRTC** is a powerful technology for building real-time video and audio streaming applications, enabling peer-to-peer communication directly between browsers without requiring additional plugins or software.
- The **signaling server** (implemented with **Socket.io**) plays a crucial role in exchanging connection metadata, such as offers, answers, and ICE candidates, to establish peer connections.
- In the **video call application example**, we used **WebRTC** to create a simple but effective peer-to-peer video call system. You can enhance this further by adding features such as multi-party video calls, screen sharing, and more advanced error handling.

By using WebRTC and Node.js, you can create scalable, low-latency video and audio streaming applications with minimal overhead, offering real-time communication for various use cases like video conferencing, online collaboration, and live broadcasts.

CHAPTER 21

BUILDING REAL-TIME MULTIPLAYER GAMES

Building real-time multiplayer games requires an efficient way to manage communication between players, synchronize game state across different devices, and handle real-time actions with minimal latency. Node.js, with its **event-driven architecture** and the powerful **Socket.IO** library, provides an ideal framework for developing such games. In this chapter, we will explore the **concepts of multiplayer gaming in real-time**, how to implement **real-time game mechanics using Socket.IO**, and we will walk through a simple example of building a **multiplayer game**.

Concepts of Multiplayer Gaming in Real-Time

When building multiplayer games, particularly real-time games, it is essential to focus on the following concepts:

1. **Game State Synchronization**:
   o In a multiplayer game, every player needs to see the same game state, such as positions of characters, items, and objects. This requires **synchronization** of the game state across all players' devices in real-time.

231

o The game state should be updated at regular intervals and broadcast to all connected players. This ensures that everyone is on the same page, preventing inconsistencies.

2. **Low-Latency Communication**:

   o Multiplayer games require minimal latency for smooth gameplay, especially for fast-paced games like first-person shooters or racing games. A high-latency connection can cause **lag**, making the game unplayable.

   o Technologies like **WebSockets** and **UDP (User Datagram Protocol)** are preferred because they allow continuous, low-latency communication between players and the server.

3. **Client-Server Architecture**:

   o Typically, real-time multiplayer games are built using a **client-server architecture**. The server manages the **game logic**, tracks the game state, and synchronizes all players' actions. The **clients** (players) send their actions (e.g., movements, attacks) to the server, and the server broadcasts the updated game state back to all clients.

   o The server also handles collision detection, physics, and other core game mechanics to ensure fairness and consistency.

4. **Event-Driven Design**:

- o Multiplayer games often use an event-driven approach. This means the game reacts to events (such as player inputs) in real-time. These events are sent over the network, and the game state is updated accordingly.

5. **Concurrency**:
   - o Handling multiple players simultaneously without affecting performance is critical. In a multiplayer game, the server must manage the **concurrency** of different players' actions, ensuring that each player can interact with the game world without blocking others.

Using Socket.IO for Real-Time Game Mechanics

Socket.IO is a popular library for real-time communication in Node.js. It allows bidirectional, low-latency communication between the server and clients using WebSockets (or HTTP long polling when WebSockets are not available).

Key features of **Socket.IO**:

- **Real-Time Communication**: Allows the server and clients to communicate in real-time, sending and receiving data instantly.

- **Event-Based**: Socket.IO uses an event-driven architecture. You can emit events (e.g., player movement) and listen for events on both the client and server.

- **Room Management**: Socket.IO allows you to organize players into **rooms**. A room is a way to group players together for a specific game session, allowing the server to broadcast messages to only the players in that room.

- **Reconnection**: Socket.IO handles automatic reconnection, ensuring that players can resume their session if they lose connection to the server.

Example: Building a Simple Multiplayer Game

Let's walk through the process of building a **real-time multiplayer game** using **Socket.IO**. For simplicity, we'll create a basic **"player movement" game** where two players can move their characters on a shared game board.

1. **Set up the Node.js project**:
   - Initialize a new Node.js project and install the necessary dependencies:

bash

```
mkdir multiplayer-game
cd multiplayer-game
npm init -y
npm install express socket.io
```

2. **Create the Game Server** (server.js):

   o The server will handle client connections, manage the game state, and broadcast player movements to other players.

javascript

```
const express = require('express');
const http = require('http');
const socketIo = require('socket.io');

const app = express();
const server = http.createServer(app);
const io = socketIo(server);

// Game state to store players' positions
let players = {};

app.get('/', (req, res) => {
  res.sendFile(__dirname + '/index.html');
});

io.on('connection', (socket) => {
  console.log('A player connected: ' + socket.id);

  // Add new player to game state
  players[socket.id] = { x: 100, y: 100 };
```

235

```
  // Send initial player data to the new
player
  socket.emit('currentPlayers', players);

  // Broadcast new player to other players
  socket.broadcast.emit('newPlayer', { id:
socket.id, x: 100, y: 100 });

  // Handle player movement
  socket.on('move', (data) => {
    players[socket.id] = data;
    // Broadcast player's new position to
other players
    socket.broadcast.emit('playerMoved', {
id: socket.id, x: data.x, y: data.y });
  });

  // Handle player disconnect
  socket.on('disconnect', () => {
    console.log('A player disconnected: '
+ socket.id);
    delete players[socket.id];
    // Broadcast player removal to others

socket.broadcast.emit('playerDisconnected
', socket.id);
  });
});
```

```
server.listen(3000, () => {
  console.log('Server    is    running    on
http://localhost:3000');
});
```

Explanation:

- o We use **Socket.IO** to handle real-time communication.
- o When a player connects, the server adds them to the game state (`players` object) and broadcasts their presence to other players.
- o When a player moves, their new position is broadcasted to other players.
- o The server manages player disconnections by removing them from the game state and notifying other players.

3. **Create the Client-Side Code** (`index.html`):
   - o The client will allow players to control their character with the arrow keys, and it will receive and display updates from the server.

```html
html


<!DOCTYPE html>
<html lang="en">
<head>
  <meta charset="UTF-8">
```

237

```html
    <meta                        name="viewport"
content="width=device-width,       initial-
scale=1.0">
    <title>Multiplayer Game</title>
    <style>
      body { font-family: Arial, sans-serif;
}
      canvas { border: 1px solid black; }
    </style>
</head>
<body>
    <h1>Real-Time Multiplayer Game</h1>
    <canvas    id="gameCanvas"    width="500"
height="500"></canvas>

    <script
src="/socket.io/socket.io.js"></script>
    <script>
      const socket = io();
      const          canvas           =
document.getElementById('gameCanvas');
      const ctx = canvas.getContext('2d');

      const player = { x: 100, y: 100, color:
'blue' };
      const players = {};

      // Listen for current players on the
server
```

```
    socket.on('currentPlayers', (data) =>
{

    Object.assign(players, data);
    drawPlayers();
    });


    // Listen for a new player joining
    socket.on('newPlayer', (data) => {
        players[data.id] = { x: data.x, y:
data.y, color: 'red' };
        drawPlayers();
    });


    // Listen for player movement
    socket.on('playerMoved', (data) => {
        players[data.id].x = data.x;
        players[data.id].y = data.y;
        drawPlayers();
    });


    // Listen for a player disconnecting
    socket.on('playerDisconnected', (id)
=> {
        delete players[id];
        drawPlayers();
    });


    // Handle player movement
```

239

```
      window.addEventListener('keydown',
(event) => {
      if   (event.key   ===   'ArrowUp')
player.y -= 5;
      if   (event.key   ===   'ArrowDown')
player.y += 5;
      if   (event.key   ===   'ArrowLeft')
player.x -= 5;
      if   (event.key   ===   'ArrowRight')
player.x += 5;

      socket.emit('move', player);
      drawPlayers();
    });

    // Draw players on the canvas
    function drawPlayers() {
      ctx.clearRect(0,   0,   canvas.width,
canvas.height);
      for (const id in players) {
        const p = players[id];
        ctx.fillStyle = p.color;
        ctx.fillRect(p.x, p.y, 50, 50);
      }
    }
  </script>
</body>
</html>
```

Explanation:

- o   The canvas element is used to display the game.
- o   Players are drawn as colored squares, and their positions are updated in real-time based on the data received from the server.
- o   The player can move using the arrow keys, and their position is sent to the server via **Socket.IO**.

4. **Run the Game**:
   - o   To start the game, run the server:

```bash
node server.js
```

   - o   Open two or more browser tabs and go to http://localhost:3000. You should be able to see each player's movements reflected in real-time on all connected clients.

Key Features of the Multiplayer Game:

- • **Real-time Synchronization**: The position of players is synchronized across all clients in real-time using **Socket.IO**.
- • **Peer Communication**: Players' movements are communicated to the server, which then broadcasts updates to other players.
- • **Dynamic Gameplay**: The game state is updated continuously as players move around the canvas.

241

- **Basic Game Mechanics**: This example uses basic **player movement** mechanics, but it can be extended to support more complex game features like shooting, scoring, or multi-player interactions.

Conclusion

- **Multiplayer Games** require effective synchronization of game state and low-latency communication. Node.js, with **Socket.IO**, provides an excellent foundation for real-time multiplayer game development.
- By using **Socket.IO** for real-time communication, we can send and receive messages between the server and clients to update the game state as players interact with the game.
- The **simple multiplayer game** we built is just the beginning. It can be extended with more advanced features like physics simulations, AI, real-time leaderboards, and more sophisticated interactions.

Using **WebSockets** and **Socket.IO** makes it possible to develop real-time multiplayer games that are both interactive and scalable. With the foundation provided here, you can start building more complex games and scale them to support more players.

CHAPTER 22

TESTING REAL-TIME APPLICATIONS IN NODE.JS

Testing real-time applications is critical to ensure the functionality, reliability, and performance of your app. Unlike traditional applications, real-time systems often involve continuous data exchange, asynchronous events, and complex interactions between the server and clients. In this chapter, we will cover how to:

1. Write **unit tests** using **Mocha** and **Chai**.
2. Test **WebSocket** and **event-driven components**.
3. Write **integration tests** for real-time systems.

Unit Testing with Mocha and Chai

Mocha is a popular test framework for Node.js that provides flexible and powerful testing capabilities, while **Chai** is an assertion library that allows you to write expressive and readable tests. Together, they enable you to write tests for your application's logic and components.

1. **Setting up Mocha and Chai**:
    o To get started, install Mocha and Chai:

```bash
bash

npm install --save-dev mocha chai
```

o Create a directory called `test` to store your test files:

```bash
bash

mkdir test
```

o Create a basic test file, e.g., `test/app.test.js`:

```javascript
javascript

const chai = require('chai');
const expect = chai.expect;

describe('Sample Test', () => {
   it('should add two numbers correctly', () => {
      const sum = 2 + 3;
      expect(sum).to.equal(5);
   });

   it('should return the correct length of a string', () => {
      const str = 'hello';
      expect(str.length).to.equal(5);
```

```
    });
  });
```

- o   To run the tests, use the following command:

```
bash
```

```
npx mocha
```

2. This will run your tests and show you the results.

3. **Writing Unit Tests for Functions**: Let's consider a real-world example: You might have a function to calculate the area of a rectangle. Here's how you would write unit tests for it.

Function to be tested:

```
javascript
```

```javascript
// rectangle.js
function calculateArea(length, width) {
   if (length <= 0 || width <= 0) {
     throw new Error('Length and width must
be positive numbers.');
   }
   return length * width;
}

module.exports = calculateArea;
```

Test for calculateArea:

javascript

```
// test/rectangle.test.js
const             calculateArea            =
require('../rectangle');
const chai = require('chai');
const expect = chai.expect;

describe('calculateArea', () => {
  it('should return the correct area for
positive numbers', () => {
    const result = calculateArea(5, 4);
    expect(result).to.equal(20);
  });

  it('should throw an error for negative
numbers', () => {
    expect(()       =>       calculateArea(-5,
4)).to.throw('Length  and  width  must  be
positive numbers.');
  });
});
```

Explanation:

o   The first test checks if the area calculation is correct for valid input.

o The second test ensures the function throws an error if the input values are invalid (negative numbers).

Testing WebSocket and Event-Driven Components

Testing real-time systems that rely on **WebSockets** and **event-driven architecture** can be a bit tricky, as you need to simulate real-time communication and asynchronous events. Here's how you can test **WebSocket connections** and other event-driven components in a Node.js application.

1. **Testing WebSocket with Mocha and Chai**: To test WebSocket interactions, you can use a tool like `socket.io-client` for client-side WebSocket connections in your tests. You can then use Mocha to run the tests and Chai to assert the expected behavior.

   First, install `socket.io-client`:

   bash

   ```
   npm install socket.io-client --save-dev
   ```

2. **Example: WebSocket Test for a Chat App**:

   Let's assume you have a WebSocket server that allows two users to chat.

WebSocket server (using Socket.IO):

```javascript
// server.js
const http = require('http');
const socketIo = require('socket.io');

const server = http.createServer();
const io = socketIo(server);

io.on('connection', (socket) => {
  console.log('A user connected');
  socket.on('message', (msg) => {
    socket.broadcast.emit('message', msg);
// Broadcast message to other clients
  });
});

server.listen(3000, () => {
  console.log('Server running on port 3000');
});
```

Test for WebSocket server:

```javascript
// test/socket.test.js
const io = require('socket.io-client');
```

```javascript
const http = require('http');
const socketIo = require('socket.io');
const chai = require('chai');
const expect = chai.expect;

describe('WebSocket server', function () {
  let server;
  let clientSocket;
  let serverSocket;

  before((done) => {
    // Set up the server
    const             httpServer             =
http.createServer();
    const ioServer = socketIo(httpServer);

    ioServer.on('connection', (socket) =>
{
      serverSocket = socket;
      done(); // Indicate that the server
is ready
    });

    server = httpServer.listen(3000);
  });

  after(() => {
    server.close(); // Close server after
tests
```

```
  });

  it('should allow messages to be sent and
received', (done) => {
    // Create a client socket
    clientSocket                              =
io.connect('http://localhost:3000');

    // Test the client sending a message
    clientSocket.emit('message',    'Hello,
world!');

    // Listen for the message broadcasted
by the server
    serverSocket.on('message', (msg) => {
      expect(msg).to.equal('Hello,
world!');
      done();
    });
  });
});
```

Explanation:

- o   The **before** hook sets up a WebSocket server and listens for connections.
- o   The **it** test case simulates sending a message from the client and asserts that the server receives the same message.

o **Socket.io-client** is used to create a WebSocket client for testing.

Writing Integration Tests for Real-Time Systems

Integration tests verify that different components of your real-time system (e.g., WebSocket server, database, APIs) work together as expected. These tests are typically run to validate end-to-end functionality in a fully integrated system.

1. **Testing WebSocket with Database Integration**: Let's build an example where a WebSocket server is connected to a database (e.g., saving chat messages to a MongoDB database).

   WebSocket server with MongoDB integration:

   javascript

   ```javascript
   // server.js
   const http = require('http');
   const socketIo = require('socket.io');
   const mongoose = require('mongoose');
   const            ChatMessage         =
   require('./models/ChatMessage');

   mongoose.connect('mongodb://localhost/cha
   tapp',      {      useNewUrlParser:      true,
   useUnifiedTopology: true });
   ```

```javascript
const server = http.createServer();
const io = socketIo(server);

io.on('connection', (socket) => {
  socket.on('message', (msg) => {
    const chatMessage = new ChatMessage({
text: msg });
    chatMessage.save()
      .then(() => io.emit('message', msg))
// Broadcast message to all clients
      .catch((err) => console.error(err));
  });
});

server.listen(3000, () => {
  console.log('Server   running   on   port
3000');
});
```

Test: WebSocket and Database Integration:

```
javascript
```

```javascript
// test/integration.test.js
const io = require('socket.io-client');
const http = require('http');
const mongoose = require('mongoose');
const socketIo = require('socket.io');
const expect = require('chai').expect;
```

```
const            ChatMessage          =
require('../models/ChatMessage');

describe('WebSocket      with      Database
Integration', function () {
  let server;
  let clientSocket;
  let serverSocket;

  before((done) => {
    const          httpServer          =
http.createServer();
    const ioServer = socketIo(httpServer);

    ioServer.on('connection', (socket) =>
{
      serverSocket = socket;
      done();
    });

    server = httpServer.listen(3000);

mongoose.connect('mongodb://localhost/cha
tapp',     {      useNewUrlParser:      true,
useUnifiedTopology: true });
  });

  after((done) => {
    mongoose.connection.close();
```

```
    server.close(done);
  });


  it('should   save   the   message   to   the
database and broadcast it', (done) => {
    clientSocket                        =
io.connect('http://localhost:3000');


    // Listen for the broadcasted message
    clientSocket.on('message', (msg) => {
      expect(msg).to.equal('Hello      from
client!');
      // Check if the message was saved to
the database
      ChatMessage.findOne({ text: msg })
        .then((message) => {
          expect(message).to.not.be.null;
          done();
        })
        .catch((err) => done(err));
    });


    // Send a message from the client
    clientSocket.emit('message',    'Hello
from client!');
  });
});
```

Explanation:

o   This test checks if a chat message is saved to the MongoDB database when a user sends a message, and if the message is then broadcasted to other connected clients.

o   It uses **Mongoose** to query the database and verify that the message was stored.

Conclusion

- **Unit Testing** with **Mocha** and **Chai** allows you to test individual components and logic in your real-time application.

- **Testing WebSocket and Event-Driven Components** can be done by simulating connections, emitting events, and listening for responses using **Socket.IO-client**.

- **Integration Testing** ensures that various parts of your application (e.g., WebSocket server, database, APIs) interact correctly and perform as expected under real conditions.

By writing comprehensive tests for your real-time systems, you ensure reliability, prevent regressions, and maintain high-quality code. This is especially crucial in multiplayer games, real-time communication apps, or any application that relies on constant, live data exchange.

CHAPTER 23

WORKING WITH MICROSERVICES IN REAL-TIME APPS

Microservices architecture is a popular design pattern that decomposes an application into a collection of loosely coupled services, each focused on a specific task. Real-time applications often require continuous, low-latency communication between services to ensure a smooth user experience. In this chapter, we will explore:

1. The basics of **microservices architecture**.
2. How to implement **real-time communication between services**.
3. An example of a **chat microservice architecture** to demonstrate how microservices can be applied in real-time apps.

Microservices Architecture Basics

Microservices is an architectural style that structures an application as a collection of small, independent services that communicate over the network. Each service is designed to handle a specific business function, such as user management, payments, notifications, etc.

Key characteristics of microservices:

- **Decentralization**: Each service has its own database and data management, which promotes autonomy.
- **Loose Coupling**: Microservices are independent, so changes to one service don't directly affect others.
- **Scalability**: Since each microservice is independent, you can scale individual services based on demand.
- **Technology Agnostic**: Each service can be written in a different programming language, as long as it can communicate over standard protocols (HTTP, gRPC, etc.).
- **Fault Isolation**: If one service fails, it doesn't bring down the entire application. Other services can continue running normally.

How it applies to real-time apps:

- Real-time apps, such as chat apps or gaming systems, need to maintain state consistency across multiple services while handling high traffic and low-latency communication.
- Microservices in real-time applications can help by isolating specific tasks (like authentication, messaging,

notifications, etc.), enabling independent scaling and fault tolerance.

Implementing Real-Time Communication Between Services

In a microservices architecture, real-time communication can be implemented between services using various mechanisms. The choice of communication method depends on the specific use case of the application.

1. **Event-Driven Communication (Message Brokers)**:
    o   In microservices, communication often happens via **message brokers** such as **RabbitMQ, Apache Kafka**, or **Redis Pub/Sub**. These systems allow services to communicate asynchronously through events or messages. This is particularly useful for real-time applications where services need to react to events (e.g., a user sends a message, a new notification is created, etc.).
    o   Example: When a user sends a message in a chat app, the message service emits an event (e.g., `user_message_sent`), and the notification service listens to this event to send a real-time notification.
2. **WebSockets for Service-to-Service Communication**:

- o   In addition to **HTTP REST** APIs or **gRPC**, **WebSockets** can also be used for **bi-directional real-time communication** between services. For instance, when two services need to maintain continuous communication for real-time updates (e.g., in chat or live video streaming applications), WebSockets can be an ideal solution.

3. **HTTP Polling or Server-Sent Events (SSE)**:

- o   For simpler cases, **HTTP polling** or **Server-Sent Events (SSE)** can be used. Services can periodically poll each other for updates, or a service can push updates to another service using SSE for one-way communication.

4. **gRPC**:

- o   **gRPC** is a high-performance, open-source RPC (Remote Procedure Call) framework developed by Google. It supports bi-directional streaming, which makes it useful for real-time communication between services in microservices architectures. It's especially suitable for low-latency, high-performance applications.

Example: Chat Microservice Architecture

Let's build a **chat microservice architecture** as an example to demonstrate real-time communication between microservices. We'll split the system into several services, such as **user service**, **message service**, and **notification service**, all of which communicate with each other in real-time.

1. Service Breakdown

- **User Service**: Manages user accounts and authentication.
- **Message Service**: Handles sending, receiving, and storing messages.
- **Notification Service**: Sends real-time notifications when a new message is received.
- **Gateway Service**: Exposes an API for the front end to interact with the chat system.

2. Setting up the Environment

We'll use **Express.js** for creating each service's REST API and **Socket.IO** for real-time communication. We will also use **Redis Pub/Sub** for inter-service communication, where one service emits events, and other services listen for those events.

Dependencies:

- **Express.js**: For creating the APIs.

- **Socket.IO**: For WebSocket communication between clients and the server.
- **Redis**: For event-based communication between services.
- **Axios**: For making HTTP requests between services.

Install the necessary dependencies:

bash

```
npm install express socket.io axios redis
```

3. Message Service (messageService.js)

The **message service** will handle the logic for sending messages and publishing an event to the **notification service** when a new message is sent.

javascript

```javascript
const express = require('express');
const socketIo = require('socket.io');
const http = require('http');
const redis = require('redis');
const axios = require('axios');

const app = express();
const server = http.createServer(app);
const io = socketIo(server);

// Redis client for Pub/Sub
```

```
const pubClient = redis.createClient();
const subClient = redis.createClient();

const PORT = 3001;

// Set up WebSocket for client communication
io.on('connection', (socket) => {
  console.log('User    connected    to    Message
Service');

  // Handle message sending
  socket.on('send_message', (message) => {
    console.log('Message received:', message);

    // Publish message to Redis (event for
Notification service)
    pubClient.publish('new_message',
JSON.stringify(message));

    // Emit the message to all connected clients
    io.emit('new_message', message);
  });
});

// Listen for Redis messages
subClient.on('message', (channel, message) => {
  if (channel === 'new_message') {
    const newMessage = JSON.parse(message);
```

```
    // Forward new message to Notification
service
    axios.post('http://localhost:3003/notify',
newMessage)
      .then(() => console.log('Notification
sent'))
      .catch((err) => console.error('Error
sending notification:', err));
  }
});


// Subscribe to new message channel
subClient.subscribe('new_message');


// Start server
server.listen(PORT, () => {
  console.log(`Message Service is running on
http://localhost:${PORT}`);
});
```

Explanation:

- When a client sends a message via WebSocket (send_message event), the server publishes the message to a Redis channel (new_message).

- The **Notification service** listens for this event via Redis Pub/Sub and sends a notification to the user.

4. Notification Service (notificationService.js)

The **notification service** listens for new messages via Redis and sends notifications to users.

javascript

```javascript
const express = require('express');
const axios = require('axios');

const app = express();
const PORT = 3003;

app.use(express.json());

// Endpoint for sending notifications
app.post('/notify', (req, res) => {
  const message = req.body;
  console.log('New message for notification:',
message);

  // Simulate sending notification (e.g., email,
SMS, in-app)
  // For now, we'll log it to the console
  console.log(`Sending notification for new
message: ${message.text}`);

  res.status(200).send('Notification sent');
});
```

```
app.listen(PORT, () => {
  console.log(`Notification Service is running
on http://localhost:${PORT}`);
});
```

Explanation:

- The **Notification service** exposes a REST endpoint (/notify) to accept notifications. It processes messages sent from the **message service** and simulates sending notifications (e.g., an email or in-app notification).

5. User Service (userService.js)

The **user service** is responsible for managing user accounts and their interactions with the system.

```javascript

const express = require('express');
const app = express();
const PORT = 3002;

app.use(express.json());

// Endpoint to authenticate and get user
information
app.post('/authenticate', (req, res) => {
```

```
const { username, password } = req.body;

// Simulate authentication (In real-world,
check username and password from DB)
   if (username === 'user' && password ===
'password') {
      res.status(200).json({ userId: 1, username:
'user' });
   } else {
      res.status(401).json({    error:    'Invalid
credentials' });
   }
});

app.listen(PORT, () => {
   console.log(`User   Service   is   running   on
http://localhost:${PORT}`);
});
```

Explanation:

- The **User service** provides an authentication endpoint that validates user credentials. This is a simplified version; in a real-world scenario, you'd query a database.

6. Gateway Service (gatewayService.js)

The **gateway service** exposes a simple API to interact with the microservices (e.g., message sending, user authentication).

266

```
javascript

const express = require('express');
const axios = require('axios');

const app = express();
const PORT = 3004;

app.use(express.json());

// Proxy authentication request to User Service
app.post('/authenticate', async (req, res) => {
  try {
    const          response          =          await
axios.post('http://localhost:3002/authenticate'
, req.body);
    res.json(response.data);
  } catch (err) {
    res.status(500).json({                    error:
'Authentication failed' });
  }
});

// Proxy message sending request to Message
Service
app.post('/send_message', async (req, res) => {
  try {
```

267

```
const          response          =          await
axios.post('http://localhost:3001/notify',
req.body);
    res.json(response.data);
  } catch (err) {
    res.status(500).json({ error: 'Error sending
message' });
  }
});

app.listen(PORT, () => {
  console.log(`Gateway Service is running on
http://localhost:${PORT}`);
});
```

Explanation:

- The **Gateway service** acts as the entry point for the client. It forwards authentication and message sending requests to the appropriate microservices.

Conclusion

- **Microservices architecture** allows you to break down a real-time application into smaller, manageable services, each handling a specific responsibility. This approach makes the app more scalable, flexible, and easier to maintain.

- By using **Redis Pub/Sub**, **Socket.IO**, and HTTP APIs, we can implement **real-time communication** between microservices and ensure that each part of the system is responsive to events.

- The **chat microservice architecture** we built is just one example of how microservices can be applied to real-time applications. You can extend it with more services like user management, payment processing, and analytics.

With microservices, you can scale individual parts of your application independently and ensure high availability, making them ideal for real-time systems with high demands.

CHAPTER 24

USING DOCKER AND KUBERNETES WITH REAL-TIME APPS

In modern application development, **Docker** and **Kubernetes** are essential tools for containerization and orchestration. These technologies allow you to easily deploy, scale, and manage real-time applications, especially when dealing with high traffic or large-scale environments. In this chapter, we will explore how to:

1. **Containerize Node.js applications** with **Docker**.
2. **Set up Kubernetes** for scaling your real-time applications.
3. **Deploy real-time apps** using Docker and Kubernetes.

Containerizing Node.js Applications with Docker

Docker allows you to package your application and its dependencies into a **container**, making it portable and easy to run in different environments (local, staging, production, etc.). Containerization ensures that the app runs the same way regardless of where it is deployed.

1. **Creating a Dockerfile for a Node.js App**:

The **Dockerfile** defines the instructions for building a Docker image for your application. Here is an example of a **Dockerfile** for a simple Node.js real-time application (such as a chat app or a multiplayer game).

Step-by-step Dockerfile:

```dockerfile
dockerfile

# Step 1: Use an official Node.js image
from Docker Hub
FROM node:16-alpine

# Step 2: Set the working directory inside
the container
WORKDIR /usr/src/app

# Step 3:    package.json and package-
lock.json into the container
 package*.json ./

# Step 4: Install the application
dependencies
RUN npm install

# Step 5: the rest of the application code
into the container
```

271

. .

```
# Step 6: Expose the port that the app will
listen to
EXPOSE 3000


# Step 7: Define the command to run the
application
CMD ["npm", "start"]
```

Explanation:

- o **FROM node:16-alpine**: We're using the official Node.js image based on Alpine Linux (a lightweight Linux distribution).
- o **WORKDIR /usr/src/app**: This sets the working directory for the app inside the container.
- o **package*.json ./**: Copies package.json and package-lock.json to the container to install dependencies.
- o **RUN npm install**: Installs the app dependencies inside the container.
- o **. .**: Copies the rest of the application files into the container.
- o **EXPOSE 3000**: Exposes port 3000 (or any port your app runs on).
- o **CMD ["npm", "start"]**: Runs the application when the container starts.

2. **Building the Docker Image**:

Once the `Dockerfile` is ready, you can build the Docker image with the following command:

```bash
bash
```

```bash
docker build -t my-nodejs-app .
```

This command will create a Docker image named `my-nodejs-app`. You can then run it as a container:

```bash
bash
```

```bash
docker run -p 3000:3000 my-nodejs-app
```

Explanation:

- `docker build -t my-nodejs-app .`: Builds the Docker image using the current directory (`.`) as the build context.
- `docker run -p 3000:3000 my-nodejs-app`: Runs the container and maps port 3000 inside the container to port 3000 on your host machine.

3. **Docker Compose for Multi-Container Applications**:

When you have multiple services, such as a **Node.js app** and a **Redis** service, you can use **Docker Compose** to define and manage multiple containers.

docker-compose.yml example:

```yaml
yaml

version: '3'
services:
  app:
    build: .
    ports:
      - "3000:3000"
    depends_on:
      - redis
  redis:
    image: "redis:alpine"
    ports:
      - "6379:6379"
```

Explanation:

- This `docker-compose.yml` file defines two services: `app` (the Node.js app) and `redis` (a Redis service).
- **depends_on** ensures the `redis` container is started before the `app` container.

To run both containers, use the following command:

```bash

docker-compose up
```

Setting Up Kubernetes for Scaling

Kubernetes is an open-source container orchestration platform that helps manage containerized applications at scale. It automates the deployment, scaling, and management of containerized applications.

1. **Setting Up Kubernetes Cluster**:

   You can set up a Kubernetes cluster locally using **Minikube** or on the cloud using **Google Kubernetes Engine (GKE)**, **Amazon EKS**, or **Azure AKS**.

   For local development, install Minikube:

```bash

brew install minikube
minikube start
```

   This will start a local Kubernetes cluster on your machine.

2. **Kubernetes Manifests**:

Kubernetes uses YAML files (called **manifests**) to define the desired state of applications and resources in the cluster. Here's an example of how to deploy a Node.js app in Kubernetes.

Deployment Manifest (deployment.yml):

yaml

```
apiVersion: apps/v1
kind: Deployment
metadata:
  name: my-nodejs-app
spec:
  replicas: 3
  selector:
    matchLabels:
      app: my-nodejs-app
  template:
    metadata:
      labels:
        app: my-nodejs-app
    spec:
      containers:
      - name: my-nodejs-app
        image: my-nodejs-app:latest
        ports:
        - containerPort: 3000
```

Explanation:

- o **replicas**: **3**: Kubernetes will maintain 3 instances (pods) of the `my-nodejs-app` container, which allows horizontal scaling.
- o **selector** and **template**: Define the pod template that Kubernetes uses to create the containers.

3. **Service Manifest (service.yml)**:

A **Service** is used to expose your application to other services or the outside world.

yaml

```
apiVersion: v1
kind: Service
metadata:
  name: my-nodejs-app-service
spec:
  selector:
    app: my-nodejs-app
  ports:
    - protocol: TCP
      port: 80
      targetPort: 3000
  type: LoadBalancer
```

Explanation:

277

o **type: LoadBalancer**: Exposes the service externally (e.g., through a cloud load balancer) so that users can access the app on port 80, while Kubernetes forwards traffic to port 3000 on the pods.

4. **Deploying the Application on Kubernetes**:

   o Apply the Kubernetes manifests using `kubectl`:

   bash

   ```
   kubectl apply -f deployment.yml
   kubectl apply -f service.yml
   ```

   o You can check the status of your deployment:

   bash

   ```
   kubectl get pods
   kubectl get services
   ```

   o If you're using **Minikube**, you can access your service via:

   bash

   ```
   minikube    service    my-nodejs-app-
   service
   ```

Deploying Real-Time Apps Using Docker and Kubernetes

To deploy a real-time application using Docker and Kubernetes, follow these steps:

1. **Containerize Your Application**:
   - As previously described, containerize your Node.js real-time application using **Docker**.
   - Use Docker Compose to manage multiple containers if your application depends on other services, such as databases or caching systems.

2. **Create Kubernetes Manifests**:
   - Define **deployments** and **services** for your real-time application in Kubernetes.
   - If your app requires **WebSocket** communication or a messaging system like **Redis** or **RabbitMQ**, ensure that these components are also deployed and accessible to your application in the Kubernetes cluster.

3. **Set Up Horizontal Pod Autoscaling**:
   - Real-time applications often require the ability to handle fluctuations in traffic. Kubernetes provides **Horizontal Pod Autoscaling (HPA)** to automatically scale the number of pods based on CPU usage or other custom metrics.

Example of an HPA manifest:

```yaml
apiVersion: autoscaling/v2
kind: HorizontalPodAutoscaler
metadata:
  name: my-nodejs-app-hpa
spec:
  scaleTargetRef:
    apiVersion: apps/v1
    kind: Deployment
    name: my-nodejs-app
  minReplicas: 1
  maxReplicas: 5
  metrics:
  - type: Resource
    resource:
      name: cpu
      target:
        type: Utilization
        averageUtilization: 80
```

This autoscaler will adjust the number of pods in the my-nodejs-app deployment based on the CPU usage.

4. **Deploy to Kubernetes**:

   o After setting up your Kubernetes manifests and scaling configurations, deploy your app to Kubernetes.

```bash
kubectl apply -f deployment.yml
kubectl apply -f service.yml
kubectl apply -f hpa.yml
```

5. **Monitor and Scale**:
   o You can monitor the performance and health of your application using Kubernetes' **kubectl** commands, and scale your pods automatically with HPA.

```bash
kubectl get hpa
```

Conclusion

- **Docker** provides a lightweight, consistent environment for deploying your Node.js real-time applications. Containerization makes it easy to build, test, and deploy applications across different environments.
- **Kubernetes** offers powerful orchestration capabilities, allowing you to scale your real-time applications, manage resources efficiently, and ensure high availability.
- By using Docker and Kubernetes, you can deploy, scale, and manage real-time applications effectively, ensuring that they can handle high traffic and maintain low-latency communication between services.

281

With Docker and Kubernetes, you can easily manage the deployment of real-time apps, ensuring reliability, scalability, and performance. This is especially crucial for applications like chat systems, multiplayer games, and live-streaming services, which require constant, real-time communication between users.

CHAPTER 25

INTEGRATING NODE.JS WITH IOT FOR REAL-TIME APPLICATIONS

The Internet of Things (IoT) is revolutionizing how devices and systems interact with each other and the environment. It involves embedding physical objects with sensors, actuators, and network connectivity to collect, transmit, and process data. Real-time applications benefit greatly from IoT, as they allow businesses and developers to create systems that are not only aware of events happening in real-time but also capable of making decisions based on incoming data.

In this chapter, we will explore:

1. **What IoT is** and how it operates.
2. **How to work with real-time data** from IoT devices.
3. A practical example: **Building an IoT-powered real-time system** using **Node.js**.

283

What is IoT?

IoT refers to a network of physical objects (such as devices, sensors, and appliances) that are embedded with software, sensors, and other technologies to connect and exchange data over the internet or other communication networks.

Key characteristics of IoT:

- **Connectivity**: IoT devices are connected via networks (Wi-Fi, Bluetooth, cellular, etc.) to send and receive data.
- **Sensors**: IoT devices typically contain sensors (e.g., temperature, humidity, motion) that collect data from their environment.
- **Automation and Control**: IoT devices can be automated or controlled remotely based on the data they collect.
- **Real-Time Data Processing**: IoT enables real-time data collection, analysis, and response to events, which is critical for many applications such as monitoring, security, and automation.

Examples of IoT devices include:

- **Smart thermostats** (e.g., Nest)
- **Wearables** (e.g., Fitbit, Apple Watch)
- **Connected cars**
- **Smart home devices** (e.g., smart lights, security cameras)

- **Industrial IoT (IIoT)** sensors for monitoring machines, equipment, and supply chains

Real-Time Data from IoT Devices

The primary challenge with IoT systems is handling the real-time data that is constantly generated by devices. Real-time IoT applications require low-latency communication, rapid data processing, and the ability to make decisions based on incoming data.

Real-time data from IoT devices is usually sent to a **central server** or a **cloud platform** where it is processed, analyzed, and stored. To support real-time communication, several technologies are used, including:

1. **WebSockets**: Enables bi-directional communication between devices and servers in real-time.

2. **MQTT (Message Queuing Telemetry Transport)**: A lightweight protocol optimized for small devices and low-bandwidth, high-latency environments. MQTT is commonly used in IoT systems for real-time communication.

3. **HTTP Streaming**: For sending data in a continuous stream to the server (often used in simpler IoT scenarios).

In a typical IoT setup, the device sends sensor data, such as temperature readings, to the server at regular intervals. This data can then be used to trigger actions (e.g., turning on a fan when the temperature is too high) or to monitor the state of the device.

Example: Building an IoT-powered Real-Time System with Node.js

Let's walk through a simple **IoT-powered real-time system** where a **Node.js** backend communicates with an IoT sensor device (simulated by a simple script). In this example, we will:

1. Set up an MQTT broker to simulate communication between an IoT device and the Node.js server.
2. Build a **Node.js server** that listens for real-time data from the IoT device.
3. Display the data in real-time on a web interface.

1. Setting up MQTT Broker

We'll use **Mosquitto**, a popular MQTT broker, to handle communication between the IoT device (client) and the Node.js server. **MQTT** is lightweight and ideal for IoT scenarios where you need efficient, low-bandwidth communication.

Step 1: Install Mosquitto MQTT Broker:

- On Ubuntu, you can install Mosquitto using:

```bash

sudo apt update
```

```
sudo apt install mosquitto mosquitto-
clients
```

- On macOS, you can install it via Homebrew:

```bash
brew install mosquitto
```

- After installation, start the Mosquitto service:

```bash
sudo systemctl start mosquitto
sudo systemctl enable mosquitto
```

2. Setting up Node.js Server with MQTT

We'll create a Node.js server that subscribes to a topic (e.g., "temperature") and displays the incoming data in real time.

Step 1: Install MQTT and Express.js for Node.js:

```bash
npm init -y
npm install mqtt express socket.io
```

Step 2: Node.js Backend (server.js)

Here's the code for a Node.js server that listens for temperature data from the IoT device:

javascript

```javascript
const express = require('express');
const mqtt = require('mqtt');
const http = require('http');
const socketIo = require('socket.io');

// Set up Express app and HTTP server
const app = express();
const server = http.createServer(app);
const io = socketIo(server);

// Connect to the MQTT broker
const                    mqttClient                    =
mqtt.connect('mqtt://localhost:1883');            //
Default Mosquitto port

mqttClient.on('connect', () => {
  console.log('Connected to MQTT broker');
  mqttClient.subscribe('temperature', (err) => {
    if (!err) {
      console.log('Subscribed    to    temperature
topic');
    }
  });
});
```

```
// Handle incoming messages on the "temperature"
topic
mqttClient.on('message', (topic, message) => {
  if (topic === 'temperature') {
    const temperature = message.toString();
    console.log('Received           temperature:',
temperature);

    // Emit temperature data to all connected
WebSocket clients
    io.emit('temperature', temperature);
  }
});

// Serve the frontend (real-time data dashboard)
app.get('/', (req, res) => {
  res.sendFile(__dirname + '/index.html');
});

// Start the HTTP server
server.listen(3000, () => {
  console.log('Server           running           on
http://localhost:3000');
});
```

Explanation:

- We use **MQTT** to connect to the Mosquitto broker and subscribe to the "temperature" topic.

289

- When a message is received on this topic (representing temperature data from the IoT device), we broadcast the data to all connected clients using **Socket.IO**.

- **Express.js** serves a simple frontend where the temperature data will be displayed in real-time.

3. Frontend for Displaying Real-Time Data

Here's a simple **HTML frontend** that connects to the Node.js server using **Socket.IO** and displays the temperature data in real-time:

Step 1: Create the Frontend (index.html)

html

```html
<!DOCTYPE html>
<html lang="en">
<head>
  <meta charset="UTF-8">
  <meta name="viewport" content="width=device-width, initial-scale=1.0">
  <title>Real-Time IoT Dashboard</title>
  <style>
    body { font-family: Arial, sans-serif; text-align: center; padding: 50px; }
    h1 { font-size: 2em; }
    .temperature { font-size: 3em; color: blue; }
```

```
  </style>
</head>
<body>
  <h1>Real-Time Temperature Dashboard</h1>
  <div                    class="temperature"
id="temperature">Waiting for data...</div>

  <script
src="/socket.io/socket.io.js"></script>
  <script>
    const socket = io();

    socket.on('temperature', (temp) => {

document.getElementById('temperature').innerTex
t = `${temp}°C`;
    });
  </script>
</body>
</html>
```

Explanation:

- This simple HTML page connects to the Node.js server using **Socket.IO** and listens for the `temperature` event.
- When new temperature data is received, it updates the displayed temperature on the page.

291

4. Simulating an IoT Device (temperatureSensor.js)

To simulate an IoT device, we can create a simple **Node.js script** that publishes random temperature data to the MQTT broker at regular intervals.

Simulating the IoT device:

```javascript
const mqtt = require('mqtt');

// Connect to the MQTT broker
const                    mqttClient                =
mqtt.connect('mqtt://localhost:1883');

// Simulate sending temperature data every 5
seconds
setInterval(() => {
  const temperature = (Math.random() * 30 +
10).toFixed(2); // Random temperature between 10
and 40°C
  mqttClient.publish('temperature',
temperature);
  console.log(`Sent                    temperature:
${temperature}°C`);
}, 5000);
```

Explanation:

- This script generates random temperature values between 10°C and 40°C and publishes them to the `temperature` topic on the MQTT broker every 5 seconds.

5. Running the System

1. **Start the MQTT broker** (if you haven't done so already):

bash

```
mosquitto
```

2. **Start the Node.js server**:

bash

```
node server.js
```

3. **Run the IoT device simulation**:

bash

```
node temperatureSensor.js
```

4. **Open the frontend**: Open your browser and navigate to `http://localhost:3000`. You should see the real-time temperature updates displayed on the dashboard.

Conclusion

- **IoT (Internet of Things)** enables devices to collect, send, and receive data, making it an essential part of real-time applications. Node.js is a great choice for building real-time systems due to its ability to handle high concurrency and real-time data communication.

- In this chapter, we used **MQTT** for real-time communication between an IoT device and a Node.js backend. We built a simple real-time dashboard to display temperature data coming from an IoT device in real-time.

- This setup can be easily extended to handle more complex IoT use cases, such as controlling IoT devices, monitoring environmental conditions, or tracking assets in real-time.

By integrating **Node.js** with **IoT** and leveraging real-time technologies like **MQTT** and **Socket.IO**, you can build scalable, responsive, and interactive applications that make the most of the data coming from IoT devices.

CHAPTER 26

FUTURE TRENDS IN REAL-TIME NODE.JS APPLICATIONS

As technology evolves, so do the requirements for real-time applications. In the context of **Node.js**, several emerging trends are reshaping how we develop and deploy real-time systems. In this chapter, we'll discuss:

1. **The rise of serverless computing** and its impact on real-time applications.
2. **Edge computing** and how it influences the architecture of real-time apps.
3. The **future of WebSockets** and other real-time communication protocols.

The Rise of Serverless Computing

Serverless computing refers to a cloud computing model where developers write code without needing to manage the underlying infrastructure. The cloud provider takes care of server provisioning, scaling, and maintenance. Instead of running a full application server, serverless platforms enable developers to write individual functions that respond to events.

How serverless affects real-time Node.js applications:

- **Simplified Deployment**: Developers no longer need to worry about provisioning and scaling servers. With serverless, you deploy functions that are automatically scaled by the cloud provider, making it easier to manage real-time applications that need to respond to spikes in traffic.

- **Event-Driven Architecture**: Serverless platforms are inherently event-driven, making them ideal for real-time applications. For instance, an event like a user joining a chat room, a message being sent, or a sensor sending data can trigger a function. This aligns well with real-time systems, which rely on immediate responses to events.

- **Scalability and Cost Efficiency**: Serverless platforms, such as AWS Lambda, allow for the automatic scaling of individual functions, providing more efficient use of resources. For real-time applications, this is beneficial because you only pay for the computing time that's actually used. The system can automatically scale based on the number of incoming requests or events, such as the number of connected users or messages.

- **Challenges for Real-Time**: While serverless has many benefits, handling **low-latency**, **long-lived connections** (such as WebSockets), and **stateful connections** in a serverless environment can be tricky. Serverless functions typically have a short lifecycle, which makes managing long-lived WebSocket connections and maintaining real-time communication across multiple serverless instances a challenge. However, serverless frameworks and services are evolving to better handle these scenarios (e.g., AWS API Gateway for WebSockets).

Edge Computing and Its Impact on Real-Time Apps

Edge computing involves processing data closer to the location where it is generated, rather than relying on a centralized data center. This approach helps reduce latency, increases speed, and improves performance for real-time applications. Edge computing is particularly valuable for IoT systems, video streaming, gaming, and other latency-sensitive real-time applications.

How edge computing affects real-time Node.js applications:

- **Lower Latency**: By processing data at the edge (closer to the user or device), edge computing reduces the round-trip time to the server. For real-time applications like **multiplayer gaming**, **video conferencing**, or **sensor networks**, reducing latency is critical for providing a seamless experience.

- **Distributed Infrastructure**: Real-time applications built on edge computing often involve multiple distributed nodes or devices that handle computations locally. Node.js, known for its lightweight, event-driven nature, is a great fit for running microservices on edge devices, enabling faster data processing at the source. This approach is especially valuable in applications like **real-time data streaming**, where quick decisions must be made based on the data collected from sensors or users.

- **Improved Reliability**: With edge computing, real-time applications can continue operating even when connectivity to the central server is lost. Edge nodes can store and process data locally and sync with the central server when the connection is restored, improving fault tolerance and reliability.

- **Use Cases in Real-Time Apps**:
    - **IoT Applications**: IoT devices can send data to local edge devices for processing, reducing the amount of data sent over the network and improving response times. For instance, a smart thermostat might process sensor data locally, adjusting the temperature without needing to send data back to the cloud.

    - **Real-Time Video Streaming**: Edge computing can optimize video streaming services by reducing the load on centralized servers and minimizing latency for viewers by processing and caching content closer to the user.

    - **Gaming and Augmented Reality**: For real-time gaming or AR applications, where latency can have a significant impact on user experience, edge computing ensures that the user's interactions are processed quickly and efficiently.

Future of WebSockets and Real-Time Communication Protocols

WebSockets have long been the go-to protocol for real-time communication in web applications. However, as technology advances, other protocols are emerging to complement or even replace WebSockets in certain use cases. Let's explore the **future of WebSockets** and other real-time communication protocols.

1. **The Evolution of WebSockets**:
    o **WebSockets** provide full-duplex communication over a single connection, making them ideal for real-time apps that require bidirectional communication (e.g., chat apps, multiplayer games). However, WebSockets have limitations when it comes to handling certain use cases, such as large-scale deployments and connection management.
    o **WebSocket enhancements** are expected to improve their performance and scalability. For example, **WebSocket 2.0** could introduce improvements like better compression, more efficient error handling, and more robust authentication mechanisms.

299

2. **WebTransport**:

   o **WebTransport** is a newer protocol being developed by the W3C that aims to provide a modern alternative to WebSockets. It is designed for low-latency communication between the browser and server, using **QUIC (Quick UDP Internet Connections)** as the transport layer, which reduces connection setup time and improves overall performance.

   o **Advantages of WebTransport**:

   - **Better handling of high-latency networks**: QUIC allows faster establishment of secure connections, making WebTransport ideal for real-time applications where low latency is crucial.

   - **Multiplexing**: WebTransport allows multiple streams of data over a single connection, similar to **HTTP/2**, but with support for real-time communication. This is useful for applications that require both low-latency communication and multiple types of data being exchanged concurrently.

3. **WebRTC**:

   o **WebRTC** (Web Real-Time Communication) has been gaining popularity for real-time peer-to-peer communication, especially for video and audio streaming. WebRTC provides **low-latency communication** and allows direct browser-to-browser communication without the need for intermediate servers.

- o **Future of WebRTC**:
  - WebRTC will likely expand to support **more robust signaling mechanisms**, **advanced media processing**, and **multi-party communication**. This could make it the go-to protocol for even more real-time applications like live streaming, video conferencing, and online collaboration tools.

4. **MQTT (Message Queuing Telemetry Transport)**:
   - o **MQTT** is a lightweight, publish/subscribe messaging protocol designed for low-bandwidth, high-latency environments. It's commonly used in IoT applications, where devices need to send data to a central server or broker in real-time.
   - o **Future of MQTT**: MQTT will continue to play a vital role in **IoT** and other real-time applications where devices need to publish data asynchronously. With the growth of IoT, MQTT's lightweight nature and its ability to handle large numbers of concurrent connections

will make it a dominant protocol for **machine-to-machine** (M2M) communication.

5. **gRPC**:

   o **gRPC** is an open-source RPC (Remote Procedure Call) framework that uses HTTP/2 for communication. It supports bi-directional streaming and is ideal for microservices architectures, where services need to communicate with each other in real-time.

   o **Future of gRPC**: gRPC is expected to continue to grow in popularity for real-time communication, especially in microservices-based applications. It offers significant advantages in terms of performance, strong typing (via Protobuf), and efficient communication between services.

6. **Event-Driven Architectures**:

   o Event-driven communication is the backbone of many real-time systems. **Event-driven architectures (EDA),** supported by technologies like **Kafka**, **RabbitMQ**, and **Redis Pub/Sub**, will continue to evolve to handle real-time streaming data from various sources.

   o **Future of EDA**: Real-time systems will increasingly rely on **streaming platforms** (like Apache Kafka and Confluent) to process high-volume real-time data streams, enabling businesses to react quickly to events and gain insights from data in real time.

Conclusion

The future of real-time applications with **Node.js** will be shaped by several emerging trends:

- **Serverless computing** will allow real-time applications to scale efficiently without managing infrastructure, making real-time systems more accessible and cost-effective.
- **Edge computing** will continue to play a critical role in reducing latency and improving the performance of real-time applications by processing data closer to the source (e.g., IoT devices, users).
- **WebSockets** will remain a key player for real-time communication, but new protocols like **WebTransport**, **WebRTC**, and **MQTT** will enhance the efficiency, scalability, and flexibility of real-time apps.

Node.js will continue to thrive as a platform for real-time systems due to its **non-blocking I/O** and **event-driven** nature. By leveraging these technologies and protocols, developers will be able to build increasingly complex and scalable real-time

303

applications that meet the growing demands of users and devices across the globe.

CONCLUSION

FINAL THOUGHTS AND NEXT STEPS

As we conclude this journey into real-time applications with **Node.js**, it's essential to reflect on the key concepts we've explored, identify the next steps for your development, and provide resources for further learning to keep you updated with the latest advancements in the field. Let's dive into each aspect:

Recap of Key Concepts Learned

1. **Real-Time Applications and Node.js**:
   - o **Real-time applications** are systems where data is updated or communicated instantly, with minimal latency. Examples include messaging apps, multiplayer games, and IoT systems.
   - o **Node.js** is well-suited for building real-time applications because of its non-blocking, event-driven architecture, which handles multiple connections concurrently without blocking the event loop.

2. **Core Technologies for Real-Time Communication**:
   - o **WebSockets**: Provides full-duplex communication channels over a single TCP

305

connection, making it ideal for real-time communication in applications like chats, notifications, and live updates.

- o **Socket.IO**: A Node.js library for real-time web applications, enabling WebSocket and fallback communication for real-time communication between clients and servers.
- o **MQTT**: A lightweight protocol for real-time communication in IoT and mobile devices, designed for low-bandwidth, high-latency environments.

3. **Microservices and Real-Time Architecture**:
   - o **Microservices architecture** breaks down applications into smaller, independent services that can communicate via APIs or message brokers like **Redis Pub/Sub** or **RabbitMQ**.
   - o **Real-time communication between microservices** often involves technologies like WebSockets, MQTT, or event-driven systems using message queues to synchronize data across multiple services.

4. **Docker and Kubernetes for Scaling Real-Time Apps**:
   - o **Docker** allows you to containerize your Node.js applications and their dependencies, ensuring that they run consistently across different environments.

- o **Kubernetes** helps manage and scale containerized applications, providing automatic scaling, load balancing, and self-healing for your real-time applications.

5. **Integrating IoT with Node.js**:
    - o **IoT (Internet of Things)** allows devices to communicate and exchange data over the internet, enabling applications like smart homes, healthcare monitoring, and industrial automation.
    - o With Node.js, real-time data from IoT devices can be processed, displayed, and acted upon efficiently, using protocols like MQTT and WebSockets.

6. **Future Trends in Real-Time Applications**:
    - o **Serverless computing** enables scalable, event-driven applications with reduced infrastructure management.
    - o **Edge computing** reduces latency by processing data closer to the source, improving real-time applications' responsiveness.
    - o The future of real-time communication protocols includes advancements in **WebSockets**, **WebTransport**, **WebRTC**, and **gRPC**, providing better performance and new features for real-time applications.

307

Tips for Continuing Development in Real-Time Applications

1. **Experiment with New Tools and Libraries**:
   - Stay current with new libraries and tools in the real-time space. Explore alternatives to WebSockets like **WebTransport, gRPC**, or **GraphQL Subscriptions** for specialized real-time needs.
   - Try out new platforms for building and managing microservices and real-time systems, such as **Serverless Framework** or **Kubernetes with Istio** for managing traffic between microservices.

2. **Focus on Scalability and Performance**:
   - Real-time applications often face scalability challenges. Explore **horizontal scaling, load balancing**, and **auto-scaling** techniques using tools like **Docker Swarm, Kubernetes**, and cloud services like **AWS, Azure**, and **Google Cloud**.
   - Consider optimizing your real-time app for **low-latency communication** using tools like **Redis** for caching, **Nginx** for load balancing, and **Content Delivery Networks (CDNs)** for faster content delivery.

3. **Keep Learning and Experimenting**:
   - Stay curious and always experiment with new technologies, approaches, and patterns. Build

small projects that incorporate real-time features, and apply what you learn to solve real-world problems.

o Real-time applications require constant attention to performance, security, and user experience. Test your applications in various conditions, optimize for efficiency, and keep up with best practices for handling real-time data.

Resources for Further Learning and Staying Updated

1. **Documentation**:

   o **Node.js Official Documentation**: Explore in-depth documentation for Node.js to understand core features and libraries for building real-time applications. Node.js Docs

   o **Socket.IO Documentation**: Learn about real-time communication between clients and servers using Socket.IO. Socket.IO Docs

2. **Books**:

   o **"Node.js Design Patterns" by Mario Casciaro**: A great resource to learn more about scalable and maintainable real-time Node.js applications.

   o **"Learning WebSockets" by Jason Boyd**: This book provides a deep dive into WebSockets and real-time communication.

- ○ **"Serverless Architectures on AWS" by Peter Sbarski**: If you're interested in serverless architectures, this book will give you a solid understanding of building scalable real-time applications.

3. **Online Courses**:
   - ○ **Udemy**: Offers various courses on real-time application development with Node.js, WebSockets, and Socket.IO.
   - ○ **Coursera**: Find courses focused on real-time web applications, IoT, and cloud technologies.
   - ○ **Pluralsight**: A wealth of video courses on real-time communication, microservices, and Kubernetes for Node.js developers.

4. **Communities and Forums**:
   - ○ **Stack Overflow**: A great place to ask questions and engage with developers who specialize in real-time applications and Node.js.
   - ○ **Reddit**: Subreddits like r/Node, r/javascript, and r/webdev are fantastic for staying updated on trends and best practices.
   - ○ **GitHub**: Contribute to open-source projects or find inspiration from other developers' real-time applications.

5. **News and Blogs**:

o **Node.js Blog**: Stay updated with the latest features, improvements, and tutorials from the official Node.js team. Node.js Blog

o **Socket.IO Blog**: Follow this blog for updates, use cases, and technical articles on real-time communication. Socket.IO Blog

o **Dev.to**: A developer community with a rich selection of articles and tutorials on real-time web apps, Node.js, and more.

Final Thoughts

Real-time applications are becoming an integral part of modern web and mobile experiences. Whether it's a chat app, an IoT-powered system, or a multiplayer game, the demand for low-latency, interactive applications is growing. By leveraging **Node.js**'s asynchronous, event-driven nature, and incorporating technologies like **WebSockets**, **MQTT**, **Docker**, and **Kubernetes**, you're well-equipped to build scalable and efficient real-time applications.

Next Steps:

- **Experiment**: Build more real-time applications, experiment with new protocols, and scale them using modern tools.

- **Stay Updated**: Follow trends in IoT, microservices, and real-time communication protocols to stay ahead of the curve.
- **Collaborate**: Join developer communities and contribute to open-source real-time projects to expand your knowledge and network.

The future of real-time applications is bright, and with the knowledge you've gained in this book, you're prepared to build the next generation of interactive, scalable, and responsive applications. Happy coding!